My year of not getting sh*tfaced

MY YEAR of NOT GETTING SH*TFACED

How I tried and failed to give up alcohol and learned the joys of moderation.

PAMELA POWER

Jonathan Ball Publishers
Johannesburg • Cape Town

First published in South Africa in 2023 by
JONATHAN BALL PUBLISHERS
A division of Media24 (Pty) Ltd
PO Box 33977
Jeppestown
2043

ISBN 978-1-77619-242-7
ebook ISBN 978-1-77619-243-4

Every effort has been made to trace the copyright holders and to obtain their permission for the use of copyright material. The publishers apologise for any errors or omissions and would be grateful to be notified of any corrections that should be incorporated in future editions of this book.

www.jonathanball.co.za
www.twitter.com/JonathanBallPub
www.facebook.com/JonathanBallPublishers

Edited by Karin Schimke
Cover by Minky Stapleton
Design and typesetting by Nazli Jacobs
Printed and bound by CTP Printers, Cape Town
Set in Source Serif

For Liam
(Because apparently having a master's research report dedicated to you is Not Good Enough.)

Contents

Author's note 9

Introduction 11

Act I: I am never drinking again (May to July) 17

Act II: Okay, maybe one glass . . . (August to November) 79

Act III: . . . or even two or three glasses (December to February) 147

Act IV: Trying not to get shitfaced (March-ing on into the future) 199

Epilogue 245

Selected reading list 247

Helpline 249

Acknowledgements 251

About the author 253

Author's note

I have changed friends' names because this memoir is about my attempts to cut down on my boozing, and I didn't want to drag them into my sorry mess by using their real names. I changed them to Shakespearean names because I found it amusing (it was either that or dead pets' names), and I had a lot of fun matching names to friends. What I did find most surprising is that so many common names are found in Will's plays. I have used real names where the people mentioned are:

1. Dead
2. Public figures
3. Where I knew they wouldn't care (Bryn, I'm looking at you).

INTRODUCTION

MOTHER'S DAY

Relax. I am not about to start a poem about how wonderful motherhood is and how blessed I am to have two beautiful children. Frankly, I found the whole growing a child thing and launching it into the world a bit of a shock to the system. I discovered I was pregnant a few days before the new millennium. We had a party planned at an old varsity friend's game farm. It was going to be a blast!

Except it wasn't.

I ended up not drinking while everyone was getting off their faces, plus I had a huge fight with the Husband. It was one of those '*how dare you get off-your-face drunk and behave like a complete tit when I am with child?*' kind of fights. *Assumes Saintly Blessed Virgin Mary expression*

The interesting thing about being pregnant and breastfeeding is that that is the only time since I was a teenager that I didn't drink for any length of time.

I first drank alcohol on my paternal grandmother's farm in Ireland. I had just turned eleven, and I was with my little brother – who is actually older than me, but I call him that to differentiate between him and my big brother – and my very glam American cousin, Paul, whom I developed an immediate crush on. This was during a major family reunion and all the grown-ups had gone into town for dinner, and my lovely Uncle Ed (my father's fave brother) tossed the car keys to Cousin Paul with a grin and a wink. We found grandmother's stash of home-made wines – including dandelion – utterly disgusting, but we still drank them. I can remember the warm feeling they gave me as we gulped them down like medicine. We drank the wine then we drove the hire car up and down the driveway. I remember ramping over the speed bumps. Something I still love doing.

Obviously I wasn't tossing booze down my throat every weekend from when I was eleven. That probably only started at university, and I've been drinking steadily ever since. Except for now, when I took a year off to really examine and change the way that I consumed alcohol. I know the title was a bit of a spoiler, but that's what this book is about. However, before we start talking about my year of not getting shitfaced, we need to define what shitfaced means.

If you've ever found yourself, after a heavy night of drinking, googling 'Am I an alcoholic?' firstly, you probably need to take a good, long, hard look at your drinking habits, and, secondly, you will find yourself bewildered about what actually constitutes Having A Problem. I've done literally hundreds of these *Am I an alcoholic?* quizzes (usually when my hangover is kicking in at 3 am) and one of the questions they always ask is: 'Has your hangover ever been so bad that it's interfered with your work?'

They're kidding, right?

No, Reader, they are not kidding.

Exhibit A

It is the dress rehearsal for the dance programme at the end of my first year at drama school. We go out with the Honours' Students to the varsity pub. I drink three gins and ten tequilas. I am black-out drunk. I remember lying on the floor of Sally's car. I remember someone holding my hair back as I puke in the loos in the dressing rooms. I then go on stage – still off my face – and keep dancing towards the audience saying, 'I'm so pissed, I just had three gins and ten tequilas,'.

This is the first time I have puked from alcohol. I am mortified the next day and do not want to face the Honours students. They are sanguine – have seen it all before and are very kind.

Exhibit B

I am in the Canary Islands selling timeshare. We go out to a bar and get off our faces. I have a screaming fight with my then-boyfriend now-Husband – a.k.a Paulus a.k.a. Fossil – and am convinced that he's trying to hurt me. I run off down the road. He is getting increasingly freaked out trying to convince me that I'm imagining things. The next day I throw up in the toilet of the show house. The toilet is literally for show and cannot flush. I scurry out and leave the puke for someone else to deal with.

Exhibit C

I'm 22 or 23. We are living on a smallholding outside Pietermaritzburg, where we will eventually get married. We go out on Friday night to the local restaurant that has a bar we like to hang out at. I drink whisky, I'm not sure why. Am I trying to be sophisticated? Is it because I'm half-Irish? We get horribly drunk. The next day, I have to teach drama classes at the local technical college. It is an Indian college, and people don't drink. After class, I sit in the head's office, supposedly doing a recap of how the classes went but really just trying not to be sick. She can see (and possibly smell) how hungover I am and is not impressed with me. My also very hungover soon-to-be husband comes to fetch me. We have to keep stopping on the freeway on the way home to be sick out of the car doors.

Exhibit D

I'm 26 and have just landed a job as an actor in an educational theatre company based at the Civic Theatre in Johannesburg. This is a big deal for me. We moved up to Joburg seven months ago and despite landing an agent, it's taken me this long to get work.

We have a small, tight group of friends – four couples – all brought together by a close friend from university. We have a fantastic dinner at the one friend's parents' house. We each drink two bottles of red wine. I don't remember much about the guys that night but the girls were having a full-on bonding session.

The next day, Women's Day, is a public holiday. I drag myself to rehearsals, pretending I have a tummy bug. I must've reeked of booze so I doubt I fooled anyone.

Our director back then, Francois Theron, is now dead. So is the head of the company, Annie Barnes, and two of the actors, Hannes Potgieter and Stanley Jacobs (who died of Covid). This is a reminder that life is short.

Do I really want to spend all that time being hungover?

I can hear you saying, dear Reader, 'But this was in your twenties, I'm sure you've calmed down since then.'

Hahahahahahaha.

I wish.

So obvs that question about drinking interfering with work got a big, fat tick, but I have to say that a lot of the other questions didn't really ring any bells for me. B.

I'm not an expert but I've read a literal SHIT-TON of quitlit (memoirs about giving up the grog) and have done a lot of googling, and, it's weird, it's almost something you have to work out for yourself. Especially, if you're a grey-area drinker – as I was.

Am.

Whatever.

And if you're deciding on cutting down and perhaps pursuing moderation, you will find this is considered verboten in some circles because moderation is the word people with alcohol use disorder employ to describe their drinking. I know this because I come from a long line of alcoholics and have heard every excuse in the book. But my favourite remains:

'Oh, I just have a couple of glasses[1] of wine every night!'

Thing is, I wasn't that person who drank a shitload and pretended I hadn't.

The most I ever drank per night on a regular basis was two glasses of wine. And I mean regular glasses, I'm not talking about those glasses you can fit an entire bottle of wine into. So I needed to find a way of managing my drinking, something that worked for me. And that something was not getting shitfaced. But to start I had to define what shitfaced meant.

To me, shitfaced is not having two glasses of wine and getting a bit

1 Two bottles.

chatty. Shitfaced is being off-your-face, dancing on the tables, loving everyone, maybe crying, thinking you're super-sexy, singing into a beer bottle, room spinning, having to put one foot on the floor when you lie down, calling relatives in Australia drunk.

That was the person – the shitfaced person – I didn't want to be anymore.

Which brings me back to Mother's Day.

Mother's Day 2021 started off so well. I had brought myself a couple of presents just to congratulate myself on being a mother before the actual day. One was a gorgeous black coat from Convoy, the other was a book I was dying to read.

Then actual Mother's Day came around and I was woken up with a cappuccino and a gorgeous array of presents, plus some hilarious cards with heartfelt messages from the Husband and the offspring. I got a stunning pair of black boots and a fabulous red polo neck, which was lovely, but there were slightly too many mentions of how much I work (see other addictions) in the cards.

When the Firstborn was in grade R in around 2006, they had an assignment where they had to write what their mummy and daddy did for work. Daddy apparently washed all the clothes, made all the meals, played golf and went scuba diving (he has been scuba diving once and plays golf badly and has no idea how the washing machine works #justsaying).

And Mummy?

'Mummy works.'

I shit you not. That's all the Firstborn had to say about me. I laughed it off at the time, but I have to say it was like a knife in my heart. So, whenever I read those cards that go on about how much I work, I smile through gritted teeth.

Lunch was booked for 12.30 at our favourite restaurant in Parktown North in Johannesburg called The Local Grill, where we have celebrated so many family occasions.

This is when the wheels didn't exactly start to come off but definitely started to wobble. I ended up drinking two large glasses of red wine and a Jägermeister at the restaurant.

We finished our meal and went home. I was feeling decidedly tipsy at this point and had a little nap (there may have been snoring and drooling) before we set off for our next adventure. Lovely friend Imogen[2] had kindly invited us to a Mother's Day lunch at her place. The Husband had already made plans to go to a restaurant for lunch, though, so she said, 'no problem, join us afterwards'.

I suspect the next day she probably wished she hadn't.

2 Not her real name.

ACT I

I am never drinking again

(May 2021 to July 2021)

MAY

Thursday
DAY 4

I have started this journal to document my attempts to get my booze habit under control because of what happened on Mother's Day. Mother's Day was on Sunday, why am I only writing this on a Thursday? Because I was paralysed by a *severe* shame attack until now. Also, I just had coffee with The Westcliff Wives – a waiter once called us that because we seemed like ladies who lunch, and the name stuck – who were at said lunch and they filled me in on what happened because I DID NOT REMEMBER! Let me summarise what went down:

- ✔ Got off-my-face drunk
- ✔ Picked fight with Hamlet[3] – a man I barely knew (no, I still don't know why)
- ✔ Fell and hurt shin and hand badly while dancing
- ✔ Was super-irritating and demanded that they play all my favourite songs
- ✔ Sang loudly (and possibly out of tune) to said songs
- ✔ Danced like I thought I was starring in *So You Think You Can Dance*
- ✔ Snatched the ciggies out of the mouths of young adults present

3 Not his real name.

and blew smoke rings while declaring, 'We did not spend 15 hours pushing you out of our vaginas for you to die of lung cancer.' (Reader, our own kids were at home and I had not pushed any of the young adults present out of anywhere.)

✔ Only remembered snippets of evening. (This is called a brownout. Yes, unfortunately that sounds like a type of diarrhoea.)

✔ Had terrible shame attack but no proper hangover.

I get the worst hangovers so I should've been cheering and turning cartwheels about that bit, but I wasn't because I knew (from my excessive googling) what that meant. That I had developed some kind of tolerance to alcohol.

My alcohol consumption had definitely increased during the days of Auntie Rona.

The getting drunk bit wasn't the huge shock to me. The not-remembering was. It's not like I haven't had brownouts before, but it had been a while. I thought I had grown up a bit. Become more mature. Clearly, I hadn't. There were gaping holes in my memory of what happened that night. Also, picking fights with people? I usually lurrrrrrve people when I'm shitfaced. What was that about?

I still break out in a cold sweat thinking about it.

The Husband was kind to me and told me not to stress after I was freaking out over what I did. But I suspect that I was embarrassing, and that he is being kind. Still, he made me feel better. I hope it's not just 'cause he's rubbing his hands in glee at the thought of me quitting booze and being the designated driver?

Friday
DAY 5

That day plays on a never-ending loop in my head because although I drank a fair bit, had I really drunk enough to forget what happened?

Perhaps someone had snuck a shot of vodka into my glass of wine, I think wildly, clearly trying to find someone else to blame for my behaviour.

Maybe eye drops? Did someone add eye drops to my drink??

Cue more excessive googling

Spoiler alert: no one had snuck anything into my vino.

A brownout doesn't just occur when you drink excessively. It also occurs when you drink consistently throughout a day. And my drinking that day had been nothing if not consistent.

What I remain grateful for, and what I write in my gratitude journal, is thank God and all my ancestors that my children were not there to witness my behaviour.

The Firstborn wanted to know how I hurt my hand. I told him that it was like when he got drunk and hurt his ankle at a party. The Husband said Will D and his dad had come to the lunch later. I had no recollection of them.

Not a bad night's sleep although I wanted to pee for about two hours before I woke up. Reread a bit of Clare Pooley's *The Sober Diaries* just to keep me on the straight and narrow.

Monday
DAY 8

I think my mother drank and smoked while she was pregnant with me (although in those days, who didn't?). I did wonder if this kind of made me addicted before I was even born. Or affected my liver somehow. Because I am a cheap drunk. After one glass of wine I can already feel the effects.

Yes, I am still looking for people to blame for my boozing.

I get a shooting pain in my hand when I bend it back and my shin is horribly bruised. In fact, it has moved on from purple and is now the most glorious yellow.

Apparently, the Husband was twirling me around, and instead of grabbing his hand I went twirling off into what I suspect was a rather nice sculpture. But I'm surmising here, I really don't remember. What I do remember is my friend's daughter, Cordelia, anxiously asking me if I was okay.

Hmmm.

Getting drunk and falling over might be funny in your twenties, less so in your fifties.

I need to Do Something About My Drinking.

But what?

Am I going to quit?

Forever?

Forever is a verrrrrrry long time.

Do I drink enough to justify that? Or will I do 100 days and then see?

These are my concerns if I give up completely:

- ✔ That I will have nothing in common with my friends
- ✔ That in fact the only thing we really share is our love of partying
- ✔ That it's going to be difficult to socialise with my extended family who like a drink
- ✔ That it will affect my marriage. How can one of us not drink? That would be . . . weird.
- ✔ THAT I WILL HAVE TO DRIVE!!
- ✔ Also, I am extremely fond of wine – and prosecco
- ✔ The fear.

The driving bit is important because I have a bit of a phobia about driving.

I only got my driver's licence at 25, after about three or four attempts. I had so many driving lessons I could've got shares in the company. I also got it four days before my wedding as a present for my Husband, who at that point was thoroughly sick of driving me around.

Okay, not that sick, because I did used to drive with just a learner's licence. Another tidbit to file under Do As I Say and Not As I Do for the offspring.

I have a phobia because my parents were not what I would describe as being the best drivers around. Dad used to like to shake things up a bit by overtaking on blind rises in fifth gear while Mom would clutch on to the seat saying the rosary.

Saying the rosary and praying generally featured a lot when Dad was driving.

And Mom.

Erratic during the day, she was a terrifying night driver when she'd had a few. I remember coming home after a boozy evening at the friends who were like cousins in Harare. Mom aimed straight for a lamp post and Maudie had to jerk the steering wheel to avert an accident. This was considered hilarious at the time. I found it considerably less amusing once I had kids of my own. (Maudie, Reader, is my big sister, except that she is both shorter and much, much slimmer than I am.)

Not only do I have a bit of a phobia – not helped, I don't think, by driving in Joburg– but I battle to see at night. The optometrist cheerily informed me that this is normal at my age and no, those funky glasses with the yellow lenses won't help.

When you drink, you have an excuse not to drive. Do I really want to be the designated driver? No. I really, really don't. I can almost feel my face adopting a martyred expression, lines of bitterness forming on my face that no Botox will be able to remove.

Tuesday
DAY 9

Woke up in the wee hours of the morning feeling sad and anxious. Booze was defs what I was using to self-medicate. The thought of having to survive social situations/holidays with no booze and cope with drunk people while not being drunk myself is scary.

Is that the reason I started to drink in the first place – to deal with Mom's drinking? Mother was one of those I-just-like-a-couple-of-glasses-of-wine drinkers who basically got off her trolley every evening. She enjoyed box wine because it was cheap, and no one could tell how much she was drinking.

A truly lovely person – I'm talking pillar of the church, oozing with compassion and ready to give you the shirt off her back during the day – she was a thoroughly unpleasant drunk at night. It was something I always knew, that Mom had a problem with booze. Mom had a problem with booze and Dad, well . . . he was the one who probably drove her to drink.

Thirteen years older than Mom, the man made Scrooge look like an amateur. She was married to him when she was twenty and he was thirty-three and I don't ever recall them being happy. I just remember the fights, mostly about money. He used money to control her, and he could also be very cruel. He would tell her she was fat or ugly or useless, it was all done in a very ha-ha-ha way, but it wasn't funny. And if I tried to defend her, he would turn that sharp tongue on me. He also liked to flirt with the woman next door purely to make Mom jealous. We found it hilarious at the time that she could possibly think anyone would find him attractive, but now looking back I feel desperately sorry for her. Put it this way: it was no wonder she drank.

I must've been about five or six and we were at a friend's house for lunch over the weekend when Mom fainted, or more likely passed out from booze. This was not an unusual occurrence and later on we took to calling it carpet diving. Auntie Ray and Auntie Shirl told me not to worry, that Mom was just 'tired' (a euphemism I would use later for my kids when they were misbehaving.)

'No, she's not,' I insisted. 'She's drunk.'

They all laughed and thought I was adorably precocious. I was definitely precocious, not so sure about the adorable part. This was one of the first instances I remember loving making people laugh and also understanding instinctually the value of 'everything is copy' – that you can take material from your life that is in reality quite shitty, and turn it into a funny story. Which I guess is what I'm doing right now, writing this memoir. But is it funny? I'm not so sure it is. Tragi-comedy perhaps.

Having to cope with the world without my red wine overcoat is painful. I feel exposed, dealing with reality head-on.

Had a little weep during my Headspace meditation this morning. This living through a pandemic thing is not a barrel of laughs. Plus, my workload is ridiculous. I currently write or edit scripts for three shows:

Show 1 is a telenovela, but we treat it like we're writing five movie scripts a week because we want it to be brilliant. It's exhausting but exhilarating work.

Show 2 is a very traditional soapie. I have been working on it forever. It is not high quality but I have learnt so much from it from an African culture perspective.

Show 3 is a sassy and sexy soapie, and the best part is that they pay us bang on time every month.

Why do I do all this work? Because the Husband's business, Go See Do South Africa, is a tourism marketing company. Yes, dear Reader, tourism marketing in a pandemic where travel is banned. He has not earned a salary for over a year now, and as I am, technically speaking, a freelancer, any of the shows I work on could be axed at any point.

Pre-Covid, the company used to be called Brochure Management and had franchises all over the country, with brochure boards in shopping centres and hotels and other touristy places. Then Covid hit and, the day before we went into lockdown, the US parent company decided to pull out of the market and gave the Husband the company. Which was both a blessing and a curse. At the time, the parent company owned the master franchise and the Gauteng and Western Cape franchises too.

We were given all of that but had very little money to operate it, and we had no money coming in. We had to retrench a whole bunch of people, which was *horrible*. I was made a director (hilarious, I know), and the Husband has pivoted and pivoted until his head spun and has started up a whole digital arm of the company. Still, it's early days and it's very tough going.

My workload every week:

- ✔ Edit five scripts on Show 1. Scripts are around 24 pages: sometimes they are pure crapola and you have to rewrite them in the voice of a hip, young, black man, even though you are a not-very-hip, middle-aged, white woman – Twitter helps with this.
- ✔ Implement the notes on five scripts. The executive producer and the head writer give you notes on said scripts and you apply all their suggestions. Sometimes they disagree, which is difficult because both of them could fire you if you piss them off.
- ✔ Do another edit – send to head writer.
- ✔ Get five scripts back from head writer – send to channel. Channel can cancel or not renew the show, so you really don't want to piss them off.
- ✔ Implement notes from channel, production house, medical advisor, police advisor, legal advisor, and issue five final scripts. We aim to be accurate, which is why we have so many advisors. Some-

times the advisors will tell you your storyline is completely wrong, which will make you lie down on the floor and weep because it means rewrites.

- ✔ Write script for show 2.
- ✔ Write script for show 3. (Sometimes two scripts)
- ✔ Write blog (For Go See Do. My Husband made me a director, firstly in case he dropped dead from the rona and, secondly, so he doesn't have to pay me. Every week I write a blog about life, movies, TV and films and whatever the hell I come up with that week).
- ✔ Promote books/think of other blogs (This means I spend a lot of time on social media. I used to enjoy social media; it's now just work).
- ✔ Work on novel.

In addition to this I have to do the shopping for the house, deal with the eternal question of what we're going to eat for dinner and make sure the Husband and the kids are okay. I am the amateur therapist in the house; everyone comes and sits in my office and talks to me about whatever's bothering them. I love that they do it; it reminds me so much of Mom. I used to love talking to her (when she wasn't off her trolley), trying to make her laugh. I like to think I fulfil the same role in our household. It's all good when things are going well, but when everyone's going through a hard time, I start feeling like a punchbag. And don't even speak to me about the trying to come up with interesting things for dinner. That is the worst thing of all. Sometimes I stand in the meat section at Woolies, gazing slack-jawed at all the offerings, wondering what the actual fuck I'm going to buy for dinner that won't have everyone turning up their noses and complaining.

No wonder I felt the need to drink every night to try and escape.

Got home from shopping to find the water and the power off and the generator not working. I usually find a silver lining in everything. No silver lining today. Just sadness. 😢

Wednesday DAY 10

This is day ten and I'm really hoping it's the day alcohol is leaving my body. I hit such a terrible, terrible downer yesterday. I just felt like we'll be in this financial hole forever with the Husband not earning and me working all hours god sends, and never getting another novel published. That the expensive ready-made lasagne and my frozen peas would defrost because the generator wasn't working.

Also how long is this fucking power outage going to last for? I just drank two really strong cappuccinos which I don't think helped, probably made me more jittery.

I read an important chapter in Jason Vale's book *Kick The Drink . . . Easily* about giving up booze. I even highlighted it. It was something to the effect of 'This is the most important decision you could make in your life.' And I really felt the weight of that statement.

Spoke to Amy (Heydenrych – Reader, she is a famous author) on the phone this morning, she gave up booze in her twenties and rarely touches any, and if she does, she literally drinks a thimbleful. We were speaking about the shame attacks after a bender. That is something I will be really happy to leave behind. She asked me about the twelve steps, but I'm not really interested in going to AA. I don't think it fits with me. I'm sure I would start making stuff up to make myself more interesting.

> *Hello, I'm Pamela and I'm an alcoholic. Yes, I drink two bottles of vino a night and I love scoring some coke whenever I can and shagging complete strangers after being arrested. Or shagging them before I get arrested or even while I'm being arrested. Shagging them in the police van. Whatever. I'm not fussy.*

This takes me back to when we first moved to Joburg from Pietermaritzburg thirty years ago. And no, I did not shag anyone in a police van. A friend treated us to some coke as a birthday present. I was terrified it was cut with rat poison and I would keel over, frothing at the mouth, and die a horrible death. None of that happened. In fact, nothing happened, it had absolutely no effect on me whatsoever. Perhaps he was conned and it was just baking soda?

In all the quitlit I've read, coke seems to be the drug *du jour*. Many of these gals were putting away two bottles a night along with a coupla lines of coke. Then having a sleeping pill, maybe a Xanax to come down. These peeps were professionals.

I am, by comparison, an amateur.

- I have never been arrested for drinking (I mean, there's still time, but it's unlikely)
- I have never had my stomach pumped
- I have never landed up doing cocaine off the lid of the loo cistern so that I could carry on drinking
- I was not having blackouts every week
- I was not drinking two bottles of wine every night.

What I have been doing is drinking a glass or two every night and getting mildly pissed every weekend, to the point where I would often need to take headache pills the next day, and probably about twice a year I was getting off-my-face drunk and spending the next day with my head down the loo puking my guts up, fantasising about going to hospital and being put on a drip but making do with Valoid suppositories and a large supply of Energade. And obviously swearing that I was Never Going To Drink Again.

Ja, we've all heard that one before.

PSA: Valoid suppositories are God's gift to hangovers.

But that's how everybody drinks, right? We all get a bit pissed at the weekend. Every now and then we go on a bender. It's normal, riiiiiiiiight?

It might be normal but I question whether this is how I should be living my life, and, honestly, should I be doing that to my body every weekend?

I have tried before to calm my drinking down, usually after some embarrassing episode of getting off my trolley. I've also made some serious attempts at moderation. Once in about 2013 after another Mother's Day event (what is it about Mother's Day?), when I think I tried to use self-hypnosis, and another in 2019 where I gave up for three months.

In 2013, Firstborn's primary school held a Mother's Day do. It was our final year at the school, so the Grade 6 moms, who were just lovely, had put a long table for all the Grade 7 moms on the stage. We proceeded to get sloshed. I have a memory of dancing on the table with the headmistress of the junior prep, who I think wasn't so much dancing as trying to make sure I didn't fall off. There was a rumour that two gals were found making out in the ladies' loos (and no, they were not married to each other), so I comforted myself with thinking that at least I wasn't *that bad*. I think I was deluding myself. I really was that bad.

The problems with both these attempts to quit the demon drink were the following: with the first one I didn't do a long enough stint without booze, and, with the second one, I gave up for 100 days, thought, 'whew, that wasn't so bad, I'm defs not an alkie, let me carry on drinking like I always have.'

Then the pandemic hit and people started dying all over the shop and business went to hell in a handbasket and Uncle Cyril or more like Auntie Nkosazana told us we couldn't drink and I felt that rebellious, 'I will bloody drink if I want to and it's not like I'm beating my Husband up or drunk driving so let me get pissed if I want to.'

So, with the stress of everything and being told that I could not drink, I basically just started drinking more. After all, we had the most draconian booze ban, I think, out of all the countries worldwide.

Like most people, I found a friendly neighbourhood bootlegger to supply me with wine, made up weird and wonderful quarantinis (cocktails) out of the bizarre concoction of alcohol in our booze cabinet (although I drew the line at pineapple beer) and moaned incessantly about the government curtailing our freedom.

But the scary thing was that the booze ban meant that suddenly the emergency rooms were free to deal with Covid patients because they weren't clogged up with the victims of domestic violence and car accidents.

That gave me a jolt.

This is what booze really does.

The second jolt came when the booze ban was lifted, and South Africans celebrated like it was independence day or something. There was even a marching band outside the one Tops liquor store. I shit you not.

I found it as hilarious as the next person. But it also made me feel uneasy. Were we really, as a nation, that addicted?

Thursday
DAY 11

Loooooong chat with Big Sister Maudie (she lives in Vic Falls, Reader. Now that is a party town!) She told me that two girls she plays bridge with have given up booze and now smoke huge quantities of dope instead. Told her that was a lovely idea, but I was trying to get off all mind-altering substances (besides coffee). My coffee addiction is going nowhere.

Feeling very virtuous at having remembered to take reusable coffee cups three days in a row. Am expecting the Nobel Peace Prize soon for my contribution to humanity.

Started reading a book called *Sober Curious*, which really speaks to me more than the other books I've been reading because, like the author, Ruby Warrington, I can't really say that I'm an AA-level alkie. But I definitely do have an addiction to booze I need to sort out.

Maudie is also keen to cut down and has instructed me to try out the dealcoholised range of wines, because we need to have something to drink while everyone else is getting off their faces.

Will pop along to the bottle store later and check out their range.

Friday
DAY 12

Yay, yay, it's Friday! Or Friyay as it's now called. Pre-pandemic days we would head to our friends' house for RWF – Red Wine Friday. But these now happen more like once every two months as people try not to infect each other with the Roro and battle the financial effects of Covid.

Read something interesting in *Sober Curious* last night. The style, by the way, is very hey schwah, but I'm totally here for some woo-woo shit. Anyway, Ruby Warrington says that she has not said that she will *never* drink again. Occasionally, she has a drink – firstly to quell her perfectionism, secondly so that she doesn't become an irritating no-booze evangelist, and thirdly as a kind of experiment. I like that idea. Particularly being a binge drinker rather than a straight-out alkie. But possibly I would try a drink at home rather than being at a party. Because when I'm at a party there's no off button.

I too do not want to become one of those bores who used to get off my face at every social event and now is super-judgie of everyone else.

No, no, no.

I have been toying with the idea that booze keeps me compliant. It's something I witnessed in my family, specifically in the relationship between Mom and Dad. I've been putting boundaries in place left, right and centre today, and feeling quite angry about a lot of things, especially people taking advantage of me because I'm a people-pleasing perfectionist who can't say no. I'm pretty sure booze is what holds a lot of people back from escaping horrible situations and imagining a new life for themselves.

Sunday
DAY 14

On Friday night I tried dealcoholised wine. Brand DC Shiraz. Not bad. Sort of like a mix of communion wine and grape juice. Frankly, if I find a decent red wine and a decent prosecco, I won't ever have to drink again.

Aside: how delicious is communion wine? Always wanted to take an almighty gulp instead of a dainty sip, and felt slightly envious of the priest getting to have a great big glug of it at the end.

We went to Blind Tiger in Parkview – our local – for the first time since I gave up booze two weeks ago. Mavis, the legendary bartender at the establishment, was horrified that I was giving up booze. Our waiter told her I wanted a hot chocolate (thanks, Clare Pooley, for this tip).

> MAVIS: What?! Hot chocolate? HOT CHOCOLATE?
> ME *now giggling*: Mavis, I've given up booze.
> MAVIS *still bewildered*: Why?
> ME: I overdid it on Mother's Day and got out of hand.
> MAVIS: I'm also giving up booze. I'm only drinking wine.

This made me snort my hot chocolate. Three youngsters came into the pub. They started telling her a long story. Mavis eyed them suspiciously and asked them for their IDs. Again, there was a long story about them not having their IDs. Mavis was not interested. They melted away.

'Babies!' Mavis said.

I drank my hot chocolate and then had an Irish coffee without the Irish, which is rather delicious, but the coffee was so strong, I battled to sleep that night. I remembered how I used to have two drinks to keep up with Husband, so that I wasn't sitting there without a glass, but would already feel pissed after the first and would be desperately gulping down sparkling water. Alcohol is not my friend.

Paulus speaks about how he doesn't necessarily get terrible hangovers after a boozy lunch/party – just a terrible, terrible downer that he can't bear. He also speaks about his mom, who was not a big fan of drinking as her mother had been an alcoholic.

Was googling dealcoholised wines and came across infusions with CBD extract. So maybe Maudie's ideas of dope smoking are not that far off.

I'm already starting to feel so much better, but according to Ruby Warrington, the mood only really lifts after three weeks of not drinking. Roll on next weekend.

The weather is chilly and wintery today and I have no real desire to go out. I'm very happy to snuggle in my bed and watch trashy TV.

Have two pimples on my face, not sure if this is part of detoxing. It's not the usual mask-acne that has inflicted all of us during Covid.

Monday
DAY 15

We are firmly into the third wave of the pandemic here in Joburg. Vaccinations are picking up, we got through the pensioners quick-quick but there are people, under-sixties, who are trying to push in and move up the roster. Of course. It is the South African way.

I felt quite blah yesterday, lay on my bed for most of the day, not even reading, just feverishly flicking through social media. I think I was feeling down because our writing team didn't win at the SAFTAs (South

African Film and Television Awards) and not only that, they put the writing awards on the Friday night with the technical awards instead of on Saturday with the acting and directing awards. I tweeted angrily about it, but no one gave a shit. So I had that I'm-a-has-been, my-life-is-over, what's-the-point-of-it-all, kind of feeling. Tried to work on my novels but I couldn't be arsed. I have three novels I'm currently working on:

1. Has a fiendishly difficult plot that I'm trying to sort out, set in the UK.
2. One set in South Africa that I've written a quarter of, then lost interest, and
3. A group novel, the Marian Keyes book, that we haven't got around to editing.

Problem is, I'm too depressed to write.

The Husband thinks I'm burnt out. The last time I went on a proper holiday where I didn't work was 18 months ago. I was supposed to have two weeks off over Christmas, but first he got Covid and then I came down with it, so I spent my break looking after him and then being so sick myself. I was so sick I thought it was goodbye and good luck for me.

Plus, someone who shall remain nameless put clothes in the washing machine and didn't check the pockets, which were full of change and broke the new washing machine, so I ended up having to hand-wash all our clothes. We were in quarantine so I couldn't even go to the laundry. You know when things are so miserable, you can't even think too much about them, you just put your head down and get on with it?

That was me, over Christmas, bent over the bath doing washing, feeling incredibly sorry for myself and just focusing on survival. Then one of the writers on our team got Covid, went into a coma and didn't make it, and that freaked me out. I kept wondering why the hell I pulled through when someone twenty years younger than me didn't.

That's why I'm so depressed now. Because all those feelings I've been suppressing have finally started surfacing and it's not pleasant. Although is it really depression? Or is it just because things are so shit? Hard to tell.

I have suffered from depression in the past. I was formally diagnosed with postnatal depression after Roo (the Lastborn) was born although I had clearly also been suffering from it when I had had Vossie (the Firstborn), three and a half years earlier. I told my gynae I wasn't feeling so great, she rang a psychiatrist friend of hers, had a little chat and then prescribed some anti-depressants. I was too worried about them getting into my breastmilk and ditched them after five days and went to a psychologist instead, a wonderful woman called Judith Ancer. My mother was horrified that I was seeing a shrink. It's interesting the stigma around it in South Africa.

Mother: A psychologist? Why?? Rather just go chat to the priest.

Me: about what? His love of small children?

No. I did not say that.

Actually, perhaps I did. We used to love to shock my mother.

Read a brilliant article about Anthony Hopkins this morning. What a fantastic man. He's been sober for 45 years. So many people I admire don't drink.

Silver lining: at least I can say I am a SAFTA-nominated screenwriter!

Tuesday
DAY 16

Full moon last night, so I slept badly. Apparently, this is not an old wives' tale and it is true that people don't sleep as well during the full moon. I did eye the dealcoholised wine last night and thought about having a glass. Not sure why. Habit? I have also been having these 'oh, my drinking wasn't so bad' thoughts, which are apparently normal. Trouble is blacking out and not remembering what the hell you did is *that* bad. Just because other people do it, doesn't make it okay.

Did a bit of research on Anthony Hopkins last night and found out that he's estranged from his daughter, who's the same age as me. Made me admire him quite a lot less. But there's an important lesson in that. Giving up booze is not going to make my life magically wonderful; I'm not going to suddenly become a bestselling author, award-winning screenwriter, wonderful mother (please note how all the work stuff came first!!) and all-round perfect person. In fact, it's kind of only by giving up drinking that one has to start dealing with one's own bullshit. I think I began to do that when I started meditating with the Headspace app seven years ago, but the booze was actually holding me back from really sorting myself out.

South Africa is officially in the third wave of the Covid pandemic.

God alone knows how we are going to survive this financially. Go See Do is bringing in zip money, which means the Husband is earning nothing.

I just put my head down and I work.

Wednesday
DAY 17

Just wrote a very honest blog post for the Husband's company – sorry *our* company, Go See Do (I'm a director, remember!) – where I admitted that I'm fed up and depressed.

Enough is Enough

> I thought it would be interesting to live through a pandemic. It's not. I thought we'd get it under control QUICKLY, that it would last a few months and that would be it.
>
> Hahahahahaha.
>
> Here we are paddling furiously, trying to get to the shore, but knowing that it's futile as we inexorably get pulled into the horrible third wave, waiting to see how big it is and how badly we're going to be dumped and who this one's going to take from us, how many more businesses will close, how many more people will be out of work while the government dithers over vaccines, and keeps going on about vaccine nationalism which doesn't really explain why dirt poor countries have vaccinated more people than us.

Don't know about all of you, but there's just something really soul-crushing about having to face our second winter STILL in lockdown with people getting vaccinated so damn slowly that we'll have herd immunity or even herd mentality looooong before we get jabbed.

Yes, I am not in a good space. And I think that's okay. I've been doing a bit of wallowing lately, NOT getting up at 5.30 every morning to walk, NOT doing any work on my novels, NOT working on a Sunday (okay, one Sunday) but spending the day in bed watching trashy TV and eating junk food and wallowing and it's been fab.

Well, not fab exactly but perhaps it's been what I've needed to do. To acknowledge that things are not great, that people's mental health has collectively taken a bit of a knock and that it's okay to not be okay. I've been in mourning. For the life we had and the people we've lost. I have to write my dead colleague's name into the scripts I'm editing every day and I would be lying if I said it didn't get to me. He was so damn young. Why him and not me? And please don't tell me it's god's will, I can't bear that nonsonso.

But I do need to find some meaning in all of this and currently it's escaping me. I guess it's just a huge lesson in how not in control we are, how short life actually is. Like with the waves in the sea, we have to surrender, not fight it. Wear our masks, sanitize, practise social distancing and GET VACCINATED as soon as we can. You can read about my experience with Covid here at www.goseedo.co.za/say-their-names/. Believe me, you don't want it.

The good thing about all of this is that you may as well shoot your shot. Tell that person that you love them, ask your crush out, write that book, make that movie, move to the beach, travel as soon as is humanly possible. Things are so messed

> up, that who cares if you get rejected, or if you fail, you can just blame the pandemic or your Covid brain. This is your chance to do something completely crazy, to reimagine your life and how you want it to be.
>
> See, I can't help myself, optimism always wins. There's always a silver lining, even though sometimes it's only a little shimmer.

I hate admitting that I'm not doing well. It's something about being a youngest child and always trying to be the tough, funny one, the one that keeps everyone entertained. Also, we were brought up not to cry. Maudie was always considered the crybaby and I thought that was a bad thing, when in fact being able to show emotion is a strength. I do not cry in public. I mean, it's fine to shed tears over a sentimental movie or at your child's nativity play but those are easy tears. I'm talking about crying where you're actually heartbroken. I hate that. It makes me feel out of control.

I always thought it was because of Dad that I didn't like crying, but I realised a while back that my mother was not a fan either.

It was April 2009, and I had accompanied Mom to Rosebank Clinic for tests. She had all sorts of scans, and afterwards they gave us the results and told us that my mother had advanced bowel cancer and I started to cry – rather sheepishly, because I'm not the crier of the family. The nurse was terribly sympathetic, my mother was not. She said: 'Come now. Pull yourself towards yourself.'

I felt as if I was doing something wrong crying, like maybe Mom felt I was making it about me? But I do feel one does get a bit of a free pass for blubbing when you find out your mom's going to die.

Thursday
DAY 18

My meditation this morning was about how we try to run away from our thoughts and distract ourselves, maybe with porn, or social media or food – or BOOZE. I used to do that all the time. And it wasn't a lot. I would go and have two glasses of prosecco at the pub and come home. But two glasses were enough to make me feel a bit pissed. It would quell my anxiety about money or work, or my kids, and I would get this euphoric feeling that everything is actually going to be okay.

That is of course because booze makes us borrow tomorrow's dopamine and use it today, as I keep reading in the quitlit.

But drinking at the pub doesn't make things magically okay.

Guess how you really make things okay? By working on them. By bringing in more money, but you have to work more hours to bring in the cash, not sit in the pub talking about it. I thought a certain lifestyle would fall into my lap and was somewhat shocked when it didn't. Perhaps being raised under a system of racial segregation gave us that idea. That, somehow, we were special and deserved everything. We're not and we don't.

Oddly enough, my work addiction seems to have calmed down since stopped hitting the booze. I've suddenly realised there's no point. I do my work to the best of the ability, but that people-pleasing thing seems to have gone for a little lie-down.

I am definitely more snippy – I realise that's probably my dopamine being all over the place – but I'm also not prepared to take shit. Yesterday, I had to call out a young writer for not doing her work. Usually, I would stew about it all day, anaesthetise myself with a glass or two of wine at night and forget about it. But yesterday I told her it wasn't good enough and made her redo the work. It made me feel shaky and like a horrible person, but I did it anyway. I'm starting to understand how I push aside my own needs and let everyone walk all over me, supposedly in the name of kindness. But as meditation teaches us (I cannot recommend the Headspace app enough), you cannot be kind to others until you are kind to yourself. Also, is it really kindness letting people deliver sub-standard work and doing their work for them? No. You're not helping them.

The point is, you don't have to deliver criticism in a mean way. And that's where I fall down, I let things stew and stew and stew until I explode, instead of dealing with it there and then in a *firm* but kind manner.

We started walking again this morning. It's dark and freezing so we're getting up at six instead of five-thirty and doing a quick thirty-minute walk. Exercise is soooooooo important to keep all the demons at bay. Have walked through two pairs of shoes already during this pandemic.

Why are walking shoes so ugly?

One of life's little mysteries.

I started reading *The Unexpected Joy of Being Sober* by Catherine Gray last night. Instead of booze, I am now completely addicted to reading quitlit: I am going to have a complete library of these books by the time this year is up. The book starts off with her in a prison cell having been arrested for being drunk and disorderly. Her drinking is the spectacular kind, which I cannot really relate to, but the book is beautifully written and she is so damn funny. One or two things did strike a chord with me, and one of them is how alcohol makes you falsely extroverted.

It made me think of Mom.

She never wanted to go out with us when she was diagnosed with cancer and gave up the booze and the smokes. I've realised why. It made her too anxious; she didn't feel comfortable meeting other people without some alcohol in her system. That, and I think she also discovered that she was an introvert, that maybe she didn't really want to go out.

I think I'm probably much more introverted than I realise. I like to see people and go out, but I also need alone time with my books and my writing and my family and my cats.

Can you even be a writer if you don't have cats?

Two days ago I received a gift from the production house of our new show. A fabulous mug and a bottle of prosecco. Now I'm sitting here staring at this bottle of prosecco. No, not because I want to down it (okay, I wouldn't mind a glass) but it's just made me realise that this is the first time in a long time I've worked for nice people.

Lots and lots of seriously fucked-up people working in TV. We have a literal smorgasbord of narcissists with degrees in gaslighting. People who are very good at their jobs and treat their employees respectfully are to be treasured.

Friday
DAY 19

I thought about going to Blind Tiger last night while the Lastborn was at extra maths, but then realised I had too much work to do and also wanted to get a quick walk in because my back was killing me. (Readers who are young writers, do not be like me. Look after your backs!) Before, I would've been desperate to have that kir royale or glass of red wine and I would've just left the work until today. I would've had one kir royale. Maybe two. Maybe gotten pretty tipsy but probably left it at that. But pubs are for drinking, and if you're not drinking, there's no incentive to go, and then it's easy to focus on what's important.

Covid infections are over 4000 a day. Our positivity rate is over ten per cent. That's not good. I'm sure we're in for more restrictions soon. Think I'm going to hunker down and not be doing too much going out now until this horrible third wave is over. Terrible to say, but Covid is giving me a good excuse not to go out.

I saw posts from Reese Witherspoon advertising Draper James dresses and saying she's open to all those barbeque/cook out/picnic invites this summer, and I got such a pang thinking of those boozy summer parties. I'm never going to have that lovely, hazy, slightly pissed feeling again

Lies on floor and wails.

Saturday
DAY 20

The beautiful sleep promised to those who give up booze has not yet materialised. I think it's because of the coffee I'm drinking. Now it feels like two cappuccinos are almost too much for me. Yesterday I got the shakes after having two large cappuccinos at Croft & Co, our local coffee shop. After reading this last memoir by Catherine Gray (*The Unexpected Joy of Being Sober*), with all the booze and the coke, I sound pathetic. Her experiences were so extreme. She spent a night in jail, and I'm going on about having the jitters from too much caffeine!

Discovered another good dealcoholised wine last night called Zero

Percent. It tastes like a very light red wine. If I have something to drink, I don't feel as deprived.

Checked out my shin this morning: it's still yellow with bruising and has a livid red mark down it and my hand still hurts where I fell.

Good reminders of why I need to Step Away From The Booze.

Sunday
DAY 21

Supposedly I will start feeling better after today because I am now three weeks without alcohol, according to Ruby Warrington's *Sober Curious*. Let's see, because so far, I'm not on any pink cloud and I'm not sleeping any better. If anything I'm sleeping worse, because I only used to have two or three glasses at night.

But the mornings are definitely better. Also, my gall bladder is not happy because alcohol used to calm it down. I ate complete junk food yesterday. Started off with a large cappuccino, followed by bacon and egg on a white bread roll with lashings of butter, then a packet of jelly teddies, then a stick of cabanossi, then some biltong, then went to the pub for a hot chocolate, then inhaled a whole pizza and then a packet of wine gums. The only bright spot is that usually I would've drunk a couple of kir royales and a half a bottle of red wine if I were still drinking, and all I had was a glass of Absolute Zero.

I know from dieting that it's very important to have something to substitute, otherwise you won't maintain your diet. In that extreme low-carb one I did, I used to drink Tab by the bucket-load and coffee with sweeteners. My dealcoholised wine is my new Tab. I hope our local boozer starts stocking some. Must also try the CBD infusions.

It's probably worth pointing out that it was that severe low-carb diet that stuffed up my gall bladder. I don't seem to have stones, but I do have sludge and for what? I managed to lose seven kilograms and then put it all back on and then some.

That bit in Jason Vale's book about making a decision that could change the rest of my life really resonated with me. I could choose to live a different life just by giving up booze. But is the different life what I want? I do worry that a lot of my friendships are about drinking. Would we find each other that interesting without the booze? Will they find me too much of a downer, worry about me taking notes (as I have been known to do), scribbling down delicious bits of dialogue? God, I hope not. I quite like my friends; we've been through a lot together. Hopefully, this will just be about adding some sober friends to the mix, and maybe some of them will even join me in calming down on the booze front.

I'm also starting to question my caffeine intake and generally what I put in my body.

Am I turning into a bore that will rabbit on about my body being a temple?

I fear that I might be.

In writing news, Show 1 (the very high-quality one) is being received really well and it's so damn good, I want to watch it every night. How lovely to work on a show one actually wants to watch!

When I first started working at Show 2 (the very traditional one), the then producer (who has since passed away) told me to 'never watch the show' as it would make me run screaming.

He was, unfortunately, correct.

Monday
DAY 22

The Husband was shouting at Oom Cyril during the family meeting last night. As the daughter said, it was like he thought the president could hear him. When he has a few glasses of wine and I don't, we're on different wavelengths. Did have a moment of worry. Will our relationship last if he drinks and I can't?

Am I just looking for a reason to start drinking again?

Sorreeeee, I was worried my marriage would break up, so I inhaled this bottle of red wine.

Woke up with the beginnings of a migraine yesterday. Eventually took some Panado, which seemed to dampen it a bit, but I woke up feeling very naus this morning. Have now taken some Disprin in case I have to take Syndol just now. (PSA: you cannot take paracetamol followed by more paracetamol unless you want to fuck your liver up.)

It's been three weeks since I took a headache pill, which doesn't sound like much except that I was popping pills a couple of times a week when I was drinking. I would often take Disprin after a drinking session or before I went to sleep (all those fab anti-inflam properties) and it stopped my hangovers from being too horrendous.

How appalling is that?

I knew all the tricks. Certain times I would have to take Valoid suppositories to stop me puking because I couldn't stop vomiting. What is fun about that?

No. This isn't the time to tell me how much you love sticking things up your butt.

I don't feel fabulous yet because it feels like my body is resetting itself. I can't drink too much coffee now. I'm sure I had a migraine from eating too much junk food on Saturday. It's like booze allowed me to do all that stuff: I'd wake up feeling off, pop a couple of headache pills, have a few strong cappuccinos and off I'd go again. And if the headache continued, I'd just pop more pills.

It's not like I was popping codeine all day long, but it was still crazy to be taking that many pills.

I am feeling very down today. Giving up drinking feels pointless when everyone around me is constantly chucking it down their throats. But Warrick[4] keeps saying, 'Oh come on, you weren't that bad.'

Maybe I wasn't snorting coke and drinking two bottles of wine a day, but for me I was that bad.

I want a different life.

4 Warrick was my imaginary childhood friend who apparently was very naughty and was always the instigator when I did something bad. If I ate the sweets I was not supposed to eat: 'Sorry, it was Warrick.' Why was he called Warrick? Absolutely no bloody idea.

JUNE

Tuesday
DAY 23

It's the first of June and the first day of winter. If you write that on Twitter, you will get a whole bunch of people correcting you and saying that actually the first day of winter is the 21st of June.

The mute button is your friend.

Watched the *Friends* reunion on Showmax last night ,which was bittersweet and full of pure nostalgia. I felt a bit sad for all of them actually. I know we're supposed to be okay with women doing whatever they want to their faces and stuffing them full of fillers and masses of Botox; my wish is that they didn't feel like they had to. Am I being a bad feminist even asking that? But I do wonder if they really want to do all that stuff, or if they are forced to, otherwise they'll be out of work. I find it very disconcerting to see. It's like an alien has taken over their bodies and it's not the real person anymore. Working in this industry, I know only too well the pressure on women to keep looking like they're 25. It's insane. Let them goddamn age!

Listening to the cast speaking about how wonderful *Friends* was made me think of Show 1 and how much I'm enjoying it. It's so nice to work on a show of this quality. And that's kinda enough for me right now. Even though our plates are full we always want more. Well, I have quite a lot at the moment.

Thunder and lightning and pouring with rain in the early hours of the morning, which is very unusual for this time of year. Our winters are usually dry and cold. Hellooooo, global warming. I read somewhere that the weather will become more extreme so Joburg will be wetter and hotter (oh, dear, sounds like a porno) and with more hectic storms, whereas the Cape will get drier.

Started reading a very interesting book last night called *The Truth About Alcohol*. It reiterates everything I've read in *This Naked Mind* and *Kick the Drink*. But it does it in a scientific way that makes so much sense.

You know that idea that when we're pissed, our true selves come out, and we tell the truth? Hence, the whole *in vino veritas* thang. It's apparently bollocks. What really happens is something to do with our prefrontal cortex that frankly I could not be arsed to explain, mainly 'cause I never took biology for matric and I will probably explain it wrong. What it means, though, is that alcohol removes our filter, it reduces us to our basest, most primitive selves. So you just say whatever the hell comes into your head without really considering whether you should be saying it. So it's not our true selves coming out. It's our most ignoble selves.

You might have noticed how when certain people get hammered, suddenly they want to tell you a few home truths or get snippy with you? And you think, 'Woah! Where did that come from?'

That's their filter being removed.

And that's why on *that day* I felt the need to pick a fight with Hamlet, the man I barely knew. He probably said something that got up my nose. Usually (that is, when I wasn't shitfaced) I would've responded with humour or perhaps just ignored him, but with no filter I thought I would just say whatever came into my head.

And no, I still can't remember what I said. All I can say is that it's pretty jolly rude to go to someone else's house and start picking fights with their guests.

Jason also mentions in his book how one relies more on stimulants when one is drinking, which explains exactly why I can't cope with as much caffeine anymore. Eventually I took Syndol last night for my headache and slept for nine hours. Am feeling a lot more reasonable this morning.

Gives up alcohol, moves on to codeine!

Nah, I don't think I could be a codeine addict; the constipation alone would be enough to put me off.

The Husband admitted that perhaps he needs to give booze a swerve as it's contributing to his general feeling of depression. We are in the last push as far as the war on Covid is concerned and all of us are feeling it. Freezing today and for the rest of the week, and of course in the midst of this, we have loadshedding. Tra la!

Also, Melville, and the hospitals have had no water for three days. People are moaning on social media, irritable and tetchy, but also there is real pain behind the moans – and the anxiety when they do get Covid. Not knowing if it's going to kill them or one of their loved ones. No wonder we are all feeling miserable.

Beatrice (she's my helper, Reader) lost her best friend, Rosie, to Covid. They said Rosie couldn't breathe, blamed her asthma – but am pretty sure it was Covid. So sad. Bea can't even be with her friends to grieve.

Wednesday
DAY 24

It's not actually that difficult to stay off the booze at home. What's difficult is doing it when we're out and at social events. The problem also is that you avoid social events because you don't want to be faced with the temptation *or* be thought of as boring *or* find everyone else beyond irritating and become just a touch sanctimonious as you down your sparkling water.

Covid is helping me in that respect because I can just say, 'Oh, I'm worried about the third wave', and it's a great excuse to not go out. And it's not that I'm kidding. I *am* worried about the third wave. I am the only one bringing in any cash in this household. I cannot afford to get sick.

Although if I get really sick and die . . .

My life insurance is awesome. Best not to mention that to the kids.

Don't want a Menendez brothers' situation. I'm not saying the kids would take a shotgun to me and their dad if they found out how much we're worth dead, I just don't want to put temptation in their way. Perhaps I'm giving myself airs, but I do think the Husband and the offspring would be rather sad if I popped off, so better not get the Roro again and croak. Also, I really did not enjoy my first experience with Covid. Would rather not go down that road again.

What is tough is that the Husband has been feeling so down in the dumps the last couple of days, and I couldn't even whisk him off to the pub to cheer him up as I would usually do. (Reader, I know what you want to suggest that would REALLY cheer him up. Get your mind out of the gutter! This is a family show.)

A million people have been vaccinated here – only about 40-odd million adults to go. The unemployment rate is 43 per cent or something ridiculous. As the Husband said, 'No wonder I can't find a job.' And he laughed hollowly and said, 'At least I can blame someone else now – it's not just me being useless.'

Things are unbelievably tough.

But getting pissed and wallowing is not the answer. God knows we've tried it. Exercise and getting fit is a much better idea.

Bought two more bottles of dealc'd red yesterday from Woolies. Let's see what those are like. Had a long chat with Maudie yesterday. She says that she really, really wants to join me on the wagon, but she has to go to Lusaka for her grandson's birthday and she says she's going to need a lot of booze to cope with all the little people at the birthday party. She does make me laugh. Also, they have a very hectic social life and entertaining is part of their work. I'm not sure I'd be able to give up booze in those circumstances. Would just be too difficult.

Friday
DAY 26

Got an invite to Red Wine Friday and to a lunch this weekend. I have two deadlines tonight plus the writing I have to do for the Marian book, so I have a legit excuse for not attending.

Reader, do you remember the group novel I said I was working on? Let me explain.

Last year, before Covid hit, fabulous Irish author Marian Keyes was supposed to be coming to South Africa. I was asked to interview her at the Franschhoek Literary Festival, and three of my author friends were going to be on a panel with her at the Kingsmead Book Fair. Then lockdown happened and everything was cancelled. So the four of us – Amy Heydenrych, Gail Schimmel (Schim), Qarnita Loxton and moi – decided to write a novel about four unlikely people who form a book club with the aim of meeting Marian.

We wrote the thing and hadn't even been going to edit it when we decided to pull ourselves towards ourselves and first check with Marian if she was okay about us writing about her. Otherwise, we'd have had to change it to Chasing Lisa (Lisa Jewell – another fave of ours).

Then Schim – who is the brave one in the group – DM'd Marian on Twitter and guess what? Marian didn't just say, 'Oh okay,' she said how honoured she was and has agreed to read the novel. So now we are desperately editing it to make it worthy of Queen Marian.

Plus, Marian is a recovered alcoholic so that really inspires me.

All the people at Red Wine Friday will be the same peeps who witnessed my shameful behaviour at Mother's Day, so I kinda want to get it over with and break the ice. It is, however, going to be one degree tonight, so that makes me less keen.

I keep thinking that I could just give this whole no-boozing lark up. I mean – why not? It's just a self-imposed thing after all.

But when I have that thought, I give myself a little talking-to and buy another quitlit book and I'm okay again.

I just have to keep putting one foot in front of the other, writing a gratitude list every day, and not throwing wine down my throat!

Sunday
DAY 28

Finally got paid yesterday so I could pay school fees.

Still freezing. I have gone a whole month without booze and the memory of that terrible, embarrassing day a month ago is fading. I haven't lost much weight in the last month and my gall bladder is definitely aching a bit more. I can't drink as much coffee and I've found that hot chocolate is definitely a nice substitute, especially in this freezing weather. It was like a switch went off on the first day of winter and it's been frigid ever since, and our houses are not made for this cold. There is snow in the Drakensberg and in Lesotho, which is fabulous if you want to ski but not so fabulous for the rest of us.

Having said that, I enjoy the cold days when we can walk anytime of the day without overheating, and our walks in the morning are icy and stimulating and help ward off the depression that this third wave of Covid is bringing. Infections seem to be around the 5000–6000 mark per day and deaths are around a hundred. Once again I'm seeing Facebook posts about friends and relatives passing away. Social media becomes like the death notice section in the newspapers used to be. A writer friend lost her mom and dad within a week of each other. It was a week before they were due to be vaccinated.

Things are opening up overseas, which gives me hope that one day our lives will return not to normal but to our new normal. Beatrice had to be taken to hospital with palpitations yesterday. Rosie's death has hit her hard. She's not sick, she's grieving. What makes it worse is not being able to have a funeral or even a memorial service for Rosie.

We found out this morning that The Old Bullet has Covid. (The Old Bullet, dear Reader, is my father-in-law. I could never call my in-laws Mom and Dad; they just seemed too young.) He only went for a test because he was supposed to be having eye surgery later this week. Let's hope that his lack of symptoms mean that he will pull through. We are worried about him because he is nearly 80 and has high blood pressure. But there is literally nothing we can do.

Apparently, because I didn't go to Red Wine Friday, everyone thought the Husband and I were fighting. Hilarious! Our friends were very good about Covid protocols and made everyone sit outside around the fire pit, but as it was like two degrees, they were all freezing their asses off and the pizzas were a disaster. Iris kept sending me messages saying how much she missed me, which I thought was so kind. I, however, was very happy to be at home. I had a lovely evening with the kids – although they don't get why I'm not drinking. I suspect they're worried I'll be boring or become evangelical about giving up booze or will police their drinking too much. And they're probably right!

I found a lovely dealc'd wine that I tucked into, and got the next 20 scripts in. I slept in the spare room because we had loadshedding from 12 to 2.30 and I knew the alarm beeping in our room (as the battery ran down) would wake me up, and because I was asleep at ten, I was awake at five and started working on the Marian book. Am so proud of what we've achieved – and in a pandemic!

We went to Il Contadino in Parktown North for drinks at midday today. I had a hot chocolate, an Earl Grey and one of those carrot and ginger juices. I know Marian Keyes loves tea – I am going to be rediscovering my love of tea now that I'm off the booze. I still crave a lovely glass of red wine, but I keep focusing on how it makes me feel. And it's just not worth it.

Also, am loving not having hangovers.

I think I need to focus on fitness now. It would be really great to get in shape. Now that my body is healing from my fall (I still have a bruise on my shin and my hand is not fully recovered, eek!), I must start doing weights again, and really focusing on eating properly.

Monday
DAY 29

God, I hate Mondays.

In the past, these would be the days where I would swear I was not going to have a glass of wine, I was going to have an alcohol-free day and, come five o'clock, I would be gasping for a glass of red wine and I would push the alcohol-free day to somewhere closer to the weekend. I've now decided that I need to have a coffee date or something to look forward to on a Monday because Mondays are just so dreary. They're especially dreary in winter when summer and Christmas seem so far away.

At least the jasmine is budding. Spring is coming.

The Marian book is going well. We suddenly decided – okay, I decided –

that we should send it to overseas agents, but, as Schim pointed out, we'll have to cut the South African stuff and a lot of the 'fucks'. Then I had an aha moment. We're just publishing this for fun, so if they want us to cut things and change things, we can just say no.

We have now decided to send it to Schim's publishers, who are lovely.

Tuesday
DAY 30

A proper month. Have stopped drinking before, so a month doesn't seem like that huge of a deal.

Going to the shops later and will buy some Earl Grey and some English Breakfast tea. I love tea and, like my Uncle Kenny, who was a famous recovered alcoholic in my family (we had lots of alkies, just not many recovered ones), I will be drinking a lot more of it. I've noticed how at our social events there really aren't any soft drinks to speak of. There might be water or sparkling water and that's really it. I've often wandered around, gasping, looking for water to drink to try and alleviate the effects of the red wine.

Felt terribly anxious when this difficult person disagreed with me at work today. I did a bit of research (googling) and realise that this anxious response is typical of co-dependents. They/we take criticism to heart and think it's about them/us when it's really not. In fact, a lot of the time it's the other person's insecurity. The big challenge is not to react defensively or get nasty or talk about the person behind their back, but to hold firm to your own position if you really believe it – but do so politely. I didn't realise that there's a co-dependents anonymous. (Reader, children of alcoholics are often co-dependent. *Collins Dictionary* defines co-dependent like this: 'A co-dependent person is in an unsatisfactory relationship with someone who is ill or an addict, but does not want the relationship to end.')

Did some more research and read through their twelve steps; they didn't resonate. I think meditation and saying 'no' more often is going to help me, along with feeling it's okay for people not to agree with me or like me.

No, no, no, no!

I hate the thought of people not liking me. I'm like Sally Field at the Oscars: 'You love me, you really love me.'

Someone, take the internet away from me and make me work!

Wednesday
DAY 31

Polar bear weather in Joburg.

I went to bed last night having imaginary arguments with the difficult person in my head. The thing about giving up hooch is that you have to sit with these uncomfortable feelings. You can't numb them with alcohol anymore.

I also read that co-dependents use work to escape. That is me all over. Work soothes me. Maybe I should try soothing myself with some work instead of more googling.

Thursday
DAY 32

I am officially into my second month of not drinking. Woo-hoo!

Celebration with the Fab Four because Schim's publisher has agreed to read our book!

I had celebratory biccies, then I had a terrible yen for toasted cheese for lunch. It got too late for the Husband to start cooking supper, and I had scripts to get in, so we ate pizza. Had a terrible stomach ache. So bad I took two Panados at around midnight.

Wondered what the hell that was about? Is it because I've started drinking Earl Grey tea again? Or is my stomach now healing after being off the grog? After a bit of googling decided that it has to do with intermittent fasting, which is how I've been eating for more than six months now, and my stomach not being able to cope with all that food. And yes, when I'm drinking I can. But my system feels more sensitive now. I'm more aware of what I put in my body, and I can't just eat ravenously like I do when I'm a bit pissed.

Ended up having a good meeting at work – even though the difficult one was there – because I spent most of the time listening instead of performing. (Reader, I trained as an actor, and sadly that need to entertain is always there.) Reminded myself that when I do find something irritating about someone else, I need to work out why they irritate me. Quite often it will be because I share similar traits with them, which is not a very nice thing to have to admit but is very useful to know. The difficult one is a know-it-all. I have know-it-all tendencies myself.

My skin has been breaking out. Zits all over my nose. Read something somewhere that this is normal, it's just your body detoxing. God, I really hope so. Why would one have to go through more adolescent bad skin when you're done with menopause? Seems most unfair.

On the upside, checked the patch of eczema on my ankle and the weird white bumps on my forehead that I thought were from Covid. Gone! Felt so pleased to note advantages to quitting, because I have not seen any amazing weight loss just yet.

Also makes me more likely to stay off it.

PS. Did I mention that even my bowel movements have changed? They used to be dehydrated little chestnuts. Now they're smooth, sleek otter-like creatures. (Riveting, I know, dear Reader, and possibly a little more information than anyone needed.)

Sunday
DAY 35

Read a blog where someone spoke about starting to lose weight after two months off the grog, so fingers and all other body parts crossed that that happens to me. She, like moi, was also a mild binge drinker.

Not sure I'm going to bother with dealc'd red vino next week. It's useful if I'm trying to go incognito at a do, but otherwise seems slightly pointless and rather pricey. But I do want to try the dealc'd sparkling wine, also nice sparkling water like Pellegrino.

It's interesting, because it's just a whole different mindset, to realise that alcohol has no place in my life (FOR NOW – let's not get over-excited.) Went to Blind Tiger with the Husband yesterday. Had a hot choc and a sparkling water. Feels a bit pointless for me now; I only go for his sake because pubs are for drinking booze. I know this seems obvious, but you really notice it when you're not drinking.

Really hoping my gall bladder heals. My skin is definitely looking fantastic. I'm writing a blog about my father for Father's Day. I'm not ready to forgive him yet for how he treated my mother, but I do understand why he was the way he was. I just wish my mother had left him and had a better life.

Wednesday
DAY 38

It is a public holiday today – Youth Day – but when you work in TV there are no such things as public holidays. We tend to work. All. The. Time.

I've been having more and more of those 'I'm sure I can just reset my relationship with alcohol and carry on drinking' thoughts. But the big question is 'Will I even want to?' The Husband seems very keen to keep me off the booze. Is that because:

A. He finds me irritating when I drink?
B. He feels like it helps him to drink less?
C. He wants a designated driver that's cheaper than Uber?
D. He's being a supportive partner?

I wonder. I'm not sure I want the answer.

Spoke to Maudie this morning; she said she's very proud of me.

I'm proud of me too.

There are days when all I want to do is sink into a nice glass of red wine. But I know that that feeling only lasts for a moment or two, and then the headache comes, the nausea, the night sweats, the sleeplessness, the shame attacks. It's not worth it.

Friday
DAY 40

Forty days and forty nights.

Feels very biblical. Nearly-nearly six weeks without booze.

The bottle stores are now closed on the weekend. As we drove past the local boozer, the Husband commented that there isn't the usual slew of homeless people desperately queuing for their fix. When you go off booze it does make you question the whole thing – whether booze is quite as wonderful as all the ads make it out to be. Will alcohol be allowed moving forward or will it be recognised as bad for you, just like we recognise that cigarettes are bad for us? Are we one day going to have to face the fact that we have to deal with our reality instead of wanting to get off our faces all the time?

Don't get me wrong, I enjoy getting off my face. In fact, I *love* it. But here's the thing: so often these social occasions that we're dying to attend turn out to be disappointing. And if we're not invited, we feel hurt and left out. I don't have that left-out feeling anymore. I'm grateful not to be included because then I don't have to make up some lame-ass excuse for why I can't make whatever social occasion it is, when the real reason is I'm not drinking, and I don't really want to watch everyone else getting shitfaced without me.

Posted the blog about my father, then felt worried that my siblings would object and also just felt kind of exposed writing about such personal stuff. But I guess we are only as sick as our secrets.

Father's Day

It's no secret that I did not have the best relationship with my late father. In fact, I did not have much of a relationship with him at all. I suspect that he was a sociopath. That is not the same as being a psychopath. He wasn't a Fred West. We didn't wake up to suspicious mounds of earth in the back garden of a morning. Antisocial personality disorder is a spectrum. He was not on that end of the spectrum where he could not hold down a job, but he definitely had little to no empathy, and he enjoyed being cruel. He was funny, but cruel.

When he died at the end of 2003, he had the beginnings of dementia, which only magnified some of his less pleasant traits. 'Oooh, look at that,' he said pointing to a miniature coffin on the TV. 'That would be the perfect size for your son,' referring to my baby boy, who was three at the time. Was that dementia or just his personality? Difficult to tell. I was seven months' pregnant with my daughter when he died, and I really can't say that I was sad. People kept saying to me, 'It's the shock, the sadness will come.' It's coming up to eighteen years and I'm still waiting for the sadness to hit. Don't get me wrong, it was a shock when I got the news, and I did start having Braxton Hicks contractions, but they soon wore off. The management at the TV show I was working on at the time couldn't believe how nonchalant I was about the whole thing – and took the opportunity to check if I could scribble a quick script while waiting for my flight to Bulawayo.

My father was thirteen years older than my mother. They married when she was twenty, and she had her first baby at twenty-one. They both came from very strict Catholic backgrounds, and so my mother would never have dreamed of divorcing him, although God knows she should've. I hated the way he treated her, and I have found it difficult over the years since he's been gone to think of him with anything close to compassion, which makes me feel uncomfortable as I like to think of myself as someone who believes in the power of forgiveness.

That's where books can be life changing. As I was reading *The Devil You Know*, by Gwen Adshead a few weeks ago, I felt the faintest flicker of compassion for my dad, which I think says a lot about the power of words. The author is a psychiatrist who treats violent offenders, and the way she sees things from their point of view made me think about how my father's upbringing shaped him. They say psychopaths are born and sociopaths are made.

My grandmother on my father's side had eleven children, and, unlike South Africa's mysterious decuplets, I have the family Bible to prove it. Family lore has it that she was the moneybags in the relationship and owned two farms. My grandfather was a land commissioner who was responsible for giving land back to the Irish after the war of independence. He died at the age of 54 in 1941. The country house in Ireland where they lived was called Pembrokestown House. It was filled with portraits of the royal family and my aunt was named after Princess Margaret. That seemed frankly odd to me – less Irish freedom fighter and more sell-out vibes – but there you have it.

The last time I saw the family seat was in 1979 when we visited Ireland with my parents. It was very Miss Havisham's crumbling mansion meets *Angela's Ashes,* filled with gorgeous antiques and Waterford Crystal but with rooms you couldn't go into because the floors had rotted through. I remember a Druid's Altar on the property and a wood filled with bluebells, I was also *deeply* unimpressed with the weather and kept asking why we didn't go to Durban instead. It has since been restored and was even featured on *Grand Designs, Ireland* at some point.

Grandmother (we were not allowed to call her Granny) was not what I would call an involved mother. She had wet nurses for her babies, although with eleven kids I guess who could blame her? She sent the girls to boarding school in England and the boys were taken out of school and had to work on the farm. They all hated her and were terrified she was going to leave her money to my one, somewhat alternative cousin, who moved in with her for a bit, and not to the siblings themselves.

With that upbringing, it's not surprising that my father turned out the way he did. As my Husband keeps reminding me, yes, he might've been a bit of a dick but at least he gave us all Irish passports. I think the point is that although it doesn't excuse his behaviour towards my mother or anyone else, it does explain it. And understanding why someone behaves the way they do, goes a long way to helping you to forgive them.

I was being flippant when I said that I wasn't sad when my father died (of course I was flippant – I am his daughter, after all.) When I see the relationship my own daughter has with her father, I do want to have a little pity party for myself as it's made me realise what I missed out on. Mostly, though, I feel an enormous sense of gratitude that she has such a wonderful bond with her dad. The Husband is so close to both our kids and is really involved in their lives. He ferries them around, cooks amazing meals, is teaching the Firstborn to drive (he deserves a medal just for that) and has worked his (rather sexy) ass off trying to keep this business going since Covid hit. He is a dad – and a partner – in a million.

Nan – Mom's mom – used to call my father Bullshit Bertie, which used to upset me no end because, believe it or not, I was a real Daddy's girl when I was little. It was only after I saw the way he treated Ma that I began to despise him. Nan was Afrikaans and had been kicked out of her family for marrying the French Charlie. She had also converted to Catholicism.

Charlie, who was an alcoholic, was the manager of a sugar-cane farm that was staffed with Indian workers. Grandpa Charlie used to speak fluent Hindi, and the workers would come and visit him, and they would sit on the stoep, chatting. I suspect that's why my father thought he was above my mother, because his family were landowners, and she was the daughter of a farm manager.

While I was researching (googling when I was supposed to be working) my own family history, I suddenly wondered if my granddaughter might one day want to find out more about me. That is, if I'm lucky enough to have any grandchildren. Doubtful at this point. The offspring go on and on about how awful kids are and so expensive (um . . . tell me something I don't know), so I won't hold my breath.

The third wave is going berserk. We had over 13 000 infections two days ago and nearly eight thou of those were Gauteng. So many of our friends are infected. I just pray everyone gets through it. One of the cousins is in ICU. Very hectic.

Sunday
DAY 42

It's Father's Day today – six weeks since that fatal Mother's Day fiasco. Feeling very pleased and proud of myself. Especially when I consider past Father's Days. I think it was in 2008 and we were at Cousin Kel's 35th birthday party, which means I was around 39. It was held in Melville at a restaurant that used to be next door to the video shop (remember those days!). It was a fabulous party and I got plastered and was dancing up a storm. When I went outside to get some fresh air, very clever nephew KC, who was 15 at the time, and his friend asked me to order drinks for them, and I did. Feel very ashamed of myself when I think about it, because it's not something I would've ever done if I were sober. Now I hate it when people try and force my kids to drink ('Oh, come on, they're old enough to have just one,' or, 'Another one's not going to hurt them'), but of course back then my kids were little, and I didn't think about how inappropriate it was because it seemed very removed for me. Only as my kids became teens did I realise how not okay it was.

The next day was Father's Day, and we had booked a table at a local restaurant. I kept eyeing the pot plant and wondering if I was going to have to puke into it.

But that was then.

Now I am all sober and sparkly-eyed and we are off to a Father's Day lunch where I won't have to puke into anything. The Husband and maybe even the kids will most probably get a bit tipsy.

I may find them irritating.

I may have to drive home.

I will report back later.

Later: I had a very nice virgin mojito at the steak house, but the food was disappointing. There also wasn't much of a choice when it came to non-alcoholic drink. No dealc'd wine, which is surprising considering the lockdowns we've had where no booze was allowed. We had dinner at Marble, a posh establishment in Rosebank, for the daughter's birthday in January when there was a complete booze ban at restaurants and an early curfew, and I can remember feeling so antsy and wanting to get home to have a drink. I couldn't concentrate on the amazing food because there was no booze, which frankly just felt wrong.

What I did notice today is that no one in the family drank too much because I wasn't drinking, which does make me wonder how much I was contributing to the drinking culture in the house especially seeing that the Husband decided quite a while ago not to drink during the week.

We were lucky because our kids only started drinking properly at around age 17. I say lucky because a lot of the kids at their respective schools started at around 14 or 15. We did allow the kids to have a glass of champagne from about 16. I know some people say you shouldn't let your kids drink any alcohol at all, but they will do it anyway, so I wanted to be able to keep an eye on them. Was this the right decision? I wish I knew. Actor and recovered alcoholic Rob Lowe said something to the effect of: 'All you can do is try keep your kids alive, they have to decide about their own relationship to alcohol.' I'm with him on this. None of us has the answer to how to stop kids from going overboard. You have to give them a curfew and some boundaries but without being too strict or they will just rebel anyway. Beyond that you just pray and release it to the universe.

I also had a thought while I was finishing reading my latest quitlit – *The Sober Girl Society Handbook* – that in actual fact we really do not spend a huge amount of time at social occasions during the week. It would be much harder for me if I were giving up booze as a young person and all my friends were going out to clubs every night and thrashing it up. As a middle-aged woman in the middle of a pandemic, when we can't go out much anyway, it's frankly a walk in the park.

Show 1 has a no-day-drinking policy for characters, and Show 2 has a complete booze ban; they do not show booze or characters drinking at all. It used to irritate the hell out of me – do you know how difficult it is to get characters to fall into bed together without getting drunk first? Only now am I starting to get it. How pervasive and damaging booze is and how important it was for us to show people not drinking.

Monday
DAY 43

Shortest day of the year today. It's downhill to spring from here. Noticed the first jasmine bloom while we were out walking. Covid cases in Gauteng are terrible: 8 500 infections and we are averaging 62 deaths a day.

Listened to music and had a little weep last night. Not sure what I was weeping about.

That I never had a relationship with my father?

That I'm scared that I'm like him and nothing my kids do will ever be good enough?

All of the above?

Cousin Nina and I went to the same drama teacher in Harare. We were both in a concert afterwards, and instead of telling me how good I was, my father's only comment was:

'Your cousin was very good, wasn't she?'

I was probably ten.

I never want my kids to feel like they're not good enough.

Without my red wine overcoat, I am now sensitive and cry – if not freely then at least more than I did. I can't distract myself with a trip to the pub and that euphoric feeling that a couple of glasses of wine can give you. That feeling like everything's going to be okay.

When it's not okay at all.

Tuesday
DAY 44

Had pasta with a rich cheese sauce last night for dinner and then had terrible stomach cramps and didn't get a wink of sleep. Feeling crampy and weak this morning. Have been reading some stuff that says:

1. Alcohol will have had a numbing effect on any ulcers
2. You can develop a dairy intolerance after quitting.

Think I might have a dairy intolerance. It's not severe but it definitely shows itself when I eat too much cheese. Got it when I ate a pizza the other night.

Oh well, quitting is not all sunshine and roses. You also have to deal with all the physical things you've been avoiding sorting out. Like my gall bladder, which literally responds well to alcohol and coffee – so that's what I've been feeding it.

Wednesday
DAY 45

Dreamed last night that I drank some whisky. I was in church at a funeral, that's all I can remember. Then I woke up feeling guilty.

Facebook is filled with death notices of people who have succumbed to Covid. People's businesses are collapsing. It's insane.

Just wrote what might be my last-ever script for Show 2. Have worked for them for nearly 17 years. The Lastborn was six months old when I started there.

We are having problems with the one actress on Show 1, which means rewrites.

Me *chanting*: writing is rewriting.

The Gauteng infection rate is horrible. Someone said it's like India, where people are dropping dead all over the place, which is very cheery. Woolworths was empty this morning, so was Croft & Co. People don't want to go out; they're too scared.

Friday
DAY 47

We got some good news yesterday. Schim's publisher wants to publish *Chasing Marian*! They didn't send it to a reader, but the bigwig publisher read it herself – and in record time. We are all slightly gobsmacked.

Also, I immediately felt bereft that I couldn't celebrate with champagne or prosecco. How do you celebrate good things when you don't drink? I now understand the importance of cake! In fact, I love the idea of celebrating with cake. That's how things were celebrated when we were kids.

Monday
DAY 50

Woo-hoo!

I bought some dealc'd champers yesterday called Allure. WOWZA!! Tastes just like the real thing. Very dry and delish and actually a gorgeous summer drink. But after two glasses it feels a bit pointless. Ergo, I do not drink for the taste of the alcohol but for the effect. The Firstborn tried some – enjoyed the first sip and then said 'Mm, it just tastes like off juice.'

Which is what wine is.

I am still trying to get my head around why we drink. The taste thing was a wake-up call for me. If it tastes the same, why wouldn't you drink this all the time? Because it's *not* the taste we're after? Or is it because the alcohol adds something to the taste? Whatever. These dealc'd wines and champagne are very useful for social events so that you don't look like a party pooper.

We went to Blind Tiger for a last hurrah before lockdown yesterday. I had a virgin mojito, which was nice but full of sugar and one can only drink so much of them.

Also, the lactose intolerance thing puts paid to drinking masses of Earl Grey or English Breakfast (obvs I can still have green tea).

We've gone into Level 4 lockdown again. Bottle stores are closed and there's no alcohol at restaurants for the next two weeks. The Husband hasn't stocked up so is also going alcohol-free for the next couple of weeks. At least that's the theory. I think it will do him a lot of good, mood-wise. The poor restaurants can only do deliveries, and all leisure travel in and out of Gauteng is banned.

We have sold the other vehicle for Go See Do Cape Town. Will be sending the bakkie down, which means there is no vehicle up here for the Gauteng business. I try and feel grateful that we have had these vehicles to sell so that we can keep the business going for a little bit longer. But, truth be told, we are holding on to this business with a white-knuckle death grip.

Post on Facebook from an old school chum who is now at the hospital with her hubs. They both have Covid. It's just desperate.

Tuesday
DAY 51

So the Lastborn released her first single on which she sang, played the guitar and did all the harmonies herself. It's called 'Childhood Nightmare'. I was completely blown away by it and could not help myself going a bit apeshit all over social media promoting it. There is so little good news these days that it's wonderful to have anything to celebrate. Luckily, I still had some of my dealcholised champers left, so I toasted her with a couple of glasses of that. They need to do half-bottles of it!

The words of the song are slightly concerning, and the Husband and I did hope she wasn't referring to us as her 'childhood nightmare'. Everyone's always worrying that I'm writing about them in my novels (some are concerned that I'm *not* writing about them), and now I'm getting a taste of my own medicine.

Jacob Zuma was sentenced to 15 months in jail today for contempt of court. Wonder how that's going to go down with his supporters.

Wednesday
DAY 52

Maudie's birthday today. She video-called me yesterday because she wanted to show me her hair, which looks amazing. She is 62 today and looks at least a decade younger. She said 'Oh, my poor sister!' when she heard about the latest alcohol ban, and then heaved a sigh of relief when she remembered I was off the booze. Hahahaha.

JULY

Thursday
DAY 53

Our company, Go See Do South Africa, is a year old today. Our Cape Town manager had to remind us and thanked us for keeping the company going. God knows how we've done it, but we have. I think because we both believe in it so much, and we don't want to let people down. It's such a huge, huge responsibility to have staff that need to be paid every month and to know that, if the company folds, their job options are severely limited because of the pandemic.

On the script-editing work front, I'm feeling micro-managed. This always triggers me because I am excessively conscientious and never mind the extra mile – I usually go the extra marathon. It must've been around 2005 when Auntie Ray died (wife of recovered alcoholic Uncle Kenny) and her funeral was organised for a Friday in Durban. We flew down on 1Time, so called 'cause you only ever flew on them one time. This joke turned out to be true after they had problems with the landing gear and had to dump fuel in the ocean before we landed. We were so close to the water I could see the dolphins. Not really the way I pictured having a close encounter with dolphins but, still, they were pretty. Just hope all that fuel we dumped didn't kill them.

Because I am hyper-conscientious, I had made sure I submitted my script early before I left. I had also informed the new head writer that

I was going to a funeral. She did not let this worry her and insisted on phoning me and messaging me throughout the funeral, asking where my script was.

'In your fucking inbox, you silly bitch!'

No, I did not say that, but I was furious about it and confronted her when I got back. She tried to gloss over it and to calm me down, but I never forgot her horrible behaviour. Never forgot but carried on tolerating it. Grrr. Why do I always do that?

Friday
DAY 54

Last night I tried the Lautus dealc'd sparkling wine. Deeelicious. Slightly fruity and very like prosecco, whereas the Allure is more like champagne or *méthode champenoise*. Here's the interesting thing, though: I tried a sip of the Husband's prosecco – he was celebrating the first birthday of our company – and all I could taste was the ethanol. That one sip tasted so strong, it actually repelled me. Sooooooo weird, but it also felt like a kind of victory that I enjoyed the alcohol-free sparkling wine more than the normal one.

Last night I got a real sense that I can do this, that I could possibly never drink again. I *could* . . . I'm not saying I *will*. Of course, that's probably easy to say in lockdown: the real test will be when we're socialising again. Although, there is of course the writer part of me that is interested in observing how people behave when they're tanked and I am smugly sober.

Record number of infections last night – 21.5k and deaths are just under 400 – but it's like 60 per cent in Gauteng. Somebody started having an argument on my Twitter thread about whether people should be doing walk-ins for vaccinations or not. But I'm seeing more and more reports on Twitter on how nurses won't open the vial unless there are six people, and also of vaccination stations where the nurses are sitting around waiting for people, so I almost think it's worth just going and queuing.

There are increased infections all over the world – even in countries where people are vaccinated. This is making people feel hopeless and helpless – like this damn thing will never be over. I think the thing is at some point we will just have to live with it.

PS: I still have a bruise on my shin from my infamous fall on Mother's Day. Lawd!

Monday
DAY 57
Momentous day!

I have been JABBED!

Also, have spent the weekend in bed feeling absolutely dreadful. Got jabbed on Friday. I did wrestle with the ethics of getting jabbed before the 15th, which is when the over-50s are supposed to be going for their vaccinations, but was advised by Viola (she's a rather high-powered lawyer, Reader) that it was more important for me to spread the word about vaccines and set a good example than to wait. So, off the Husband and I went. He was nervy to go to Hillbrow, so we stopped by Milpark first. When he saw the queue at Milpark, Hillbrow suddenly became a much more attractive option.

Got a bit lost getting to the Hillbrow centre, but we could park inside and there was a very small queue of people. Plus we got to sit outside in the sun. Worried about getting sunburnt but it was all good.

I used to be very, very scared of injections. Luckily, the jab didn't hurt at all. I felt the liquid going in, then got a weird taste in my mouth, but that was it.

I found the whole experience so emotional; it was like voting for the first time in the democratic elections.

I was tired and felt hot and cold when I got home. Then, later that night, it was a struggle getting my shirt off – felt like I'd been kicked in the arm. Woke up in the small hours shivering and couldn't get warm no matter what I did. To add to the night's drama, the Husband fainted.

He had drunk prosecco and Savannas, which was a no-no, and yes, it was very edifying – his naked sweaty body sprawled in the middle of the passage. I kept worrying about the Lastborn coming out of her room to see what the ruckus was about and finding him inelegantly disrobed and prostrate. I draped a sweatshirt over his naked arse to preserve his modesty while I struggled to get him back in bed. (He, dear Reader, is six foot three. I am not six foot three). I stayed in bed all weekend feeling like I had a moderate case of Covid and then had horrible stomach cramps today. The vaccination site on my arm is very red and swollen.

Having experienced quite a reaction to the jab didn't really faze me because I know that I will have Gorgeous Immunity by the end of this process. Getting vaccinated gave me such a sense of hope that this shit-show might soon be over. And as the Zambian branch of the family said: it's a step closer to us being able to see each other again.

Last night the Lastborn corrected me for being politically incorrect, and I felt a surge of rage and indignation, but I remembered what my parents were like and swallowed my rage and apologised. I am, however, very aware of how selectively woke the offspring are. For example, they have no issues with someone twice their age cleaning up after them. Didn't think that was the time to point it out to them, though.

As I head to two months of sobriety, I am getting my head around the fact that the way I drink will have changed forever. That my life could be immeasurably better with this new way of being and that, in fact, I may be more me when I'm not constantly getting mildly shitfaced.

Tuesday
DAY 58

Had a very odd reaction to the video I posted about my side-effects from the vaccine on Facebook. Someone accused me of lying about what I was saying. I feel like I've made strides because I didn't take it to heart or even react to it, although at first I wanted to. After I thought about it, I realise it was his shit, not mine, and I felt embarrassed for him, particularly because he wrote 'breathe' when he meant 'breath'.

I was shocked at how old I look in the videos I made about me being jabbed. I didn't put a filter on them because I want to be more authentic.

God, yes, I really just said that.

But I mean it.

With so many dying around me, I feel like it's a fucking privilege to get old. Why should I try appearing less wrinkled or younger? I'm fifty-two, nearly fifty-three ,and I don't want to try and hide my age.

Yes, I still love make-up and looking like the best version of myself, but I frankly am more interested in how I feel than how I look these days. I do realise that one can influence the other, but I also believe that how you feel inside shines through. I feel more at peace, and I think that shows more in my face.

I want to set a good example to the offspring too. Life is not just about how you look. There are so many things that are more important than that.

I've constantly felt embarrassed about my age in the past, embarrassed to be playful or silly or to try new things because I've felt like I should somehow be beyond that. How ridiculous! I want to carry on learning until I die. I want to carry on working and doing new stuff.

I want to LIVE.

I remember when I was in first year varsity in 1986, we went to this drama party at the house of a mature student. Was it a priests and prostitutes party? Or hats and hookers? It was something like that. I dressed in sexy black underwear (as one does) and we all got legless and stripped off our costumes and jumped into the pool. They took photos of us topless in the pool, which made me cringe quite a bit later but that is not the point of this story. My main take-away from that was how much we loved the mature student. She was in her sixties – a talented actress who had finally got around to studying drama.

We should never worry about looking old or foolish.

Unless, of course, you are a complete fucking idiot.

Then you need to work on that shit.

Wednesday
DAY 59

Still have a headache after the jab and am taking Panado every day. So be it.

My thoughts today are on ego. I definitely don't feel as full of ego as when I was drinking. I don't feel the need to plaster my successes all over social media.

Am I giving quitting alcohol too much credit? I don't think so. There's something about booze that makes you generally more obstreperous and full of yourself. I now feel more introspective and filled with compassion, but also able to see people's bullshit more clearly. I understand their frailties but am also not prepared to let them walk over me anymore. If that makes sense. Maybe that's why I could let that stupid comment on Facebook about my vaccination be water off a duck's back.

I guess my boundaries are firmer, but I'm also not feeling as defensive or as 'me-me-me, what-about-me?' as I used to feel. I definitely had a sense of scarcity before – that there wasn't enough good stuff to go around and that I needed and deserved all the good stuff because I was so exceptional.

I am not exceptional. I am a reasonably talented individual who works hard and is ultra-reliable. I'm kind of comfortable with that.

The Husband and I were both discussing how people are self-sabotaging during this pandemic, making a bad situation even worse. That's what booze does. Makes a bad situation worse.

I saw on my FB Memories that the Husband bought me the first jasmine of the season on July 6th last year. God, we really thought the pandemic would be over by now. Have realised that it's not going to stop with a bang, but with a whimper.

There will be no ticker-tape parade, just a gradual petering out.

Thursday
DAY 60

Two months without booze, tralalalala!

Lockdown has definitely been my saviour. Would've not been easy if there'd been parties and lunches and book fests galore. I remember several parties I attended where I did not drink – Big Brother's 50th springs to mind, young cousin's 21st, and an event at the Firstborn's prep school. I remember feeling uneasy at them, about my own and other people's drinking. Especially the 50th because Ma got revoltingly drunk and did a bit of carpet diving (which was tricky because there were no carpets) FB memories but I remember dancing and being silly at the school event. I recall the Husband even lifting me up in the *Dirty Dancing* lift (as one does). No alcohol was necessary for that. That's going to be my next challenge – going to social events and not drinking. But the more I read and think about it, and revisit occasions where I got drunk, the more I want to leave all of that behind me.

I think I might be having the pink cloud effect that happens after you quit an addiction. It could perhaps just be a post-vaccination high, but I'm feeling in an astoundingly good mood with not much reason to be this happy. Our finances are a disaster, the Husband still has no business, just lots of promises, but I feel like there are lots of hopeful signs and that makes me feel great. He's now in the running for some European Union funding from a German company called Enpact. Not a lot – around 10 000 euros over six months – but, as he said, it will keep us going for another few months and that's all we need to be able to hang on a little longer.

I've also been reading stuff about the immunity you have if you've had one jab and a previous Covid infection and it's good news, so I'm feeling super-chuffed about that. Of the 21 000 infections nationwide yesterday, close to 500 deaths and 10 000 of the infections were in Gauteng. Our region is really suffering. Am desperately grateful to Croft and Co, where we go sit on a bench and drink coffee every morning. Makes us feel part of the world.

Monday
DAY 64

South Africa is currently burning due to the Zuma protests; his supporters were pretty pissed off and did not take well to him being locked up. Everyone's very angry and shouting about their particular point of view on the socials.

True wealth is having someone to control your social media accounts and never having to dip your toe in that particular cesspool again. Social media and drunk people: same/same. People think they can say what they like on social media; the anonymity makes them brave. Most of them are not brave enough to put their actual faces on their avatars.

Oak tree now bare of leaves and sprouting new ones. Winter jasmine coming out slowly. Smells heavenly.

Sunday
DAY 70
Mandela Day

One of the saddest weeks in recent South African history. The Zuma-related unrest got completely out of control. Malls, businesses and factories were ransacked and burnt down in KwaZulu-Natal, with 212 people dead so far. The looters swarmed the malls as if it were a race and the starter's pistol had gone off. The streets were covered in debris. People had to get out their guns to defend their houses and some went overboard and started shooting people randomly. Gunshots were going off all night. Watched people looting the blood bank during the Prez's address. That felt both tragic and utterly bizarre.

It was the worst in KZN but there was some stuff in Gauteng (pronounced 'Gwanteng' by some fool on Fox News). We've been unaffected in our part of Joburg, but Shiv heard the gunshots in Diepsloot. One of the guys in our neighbourhood set up a Dad's army to patrol our suburb, but it wasn't ever necessary, thanks god, and seemed to be a good excuse for all the men in the neighbourhood to gather at the pub to 'discuss' security concerns.

It's been a helluva week and now everyone's kind of high on rainbow-nation Kool-Aid – cleaning up for Mandela Day. Donating shit to be taken down to KZN. Insisting that the looters are not us. It was basically an insurrection-slash-coup-whatever.

Covid-wise, there will probably be a surge in cases after all the looting. Currently, we're at 300–500 deaths a day countrywide. But a million people were vaxed last week. We're up to five million vaccinated. The 35–49ers are getting out in their droves.

Monday
DAY 71

Got our contract for *Chasing Marian.*

We're getting the most fabulous advance. I am quite gobsmacked!

(Reader, let me explain what an advance is. Basically, you're given some money based on the future earnings of your book. You only then earn royalties once you have earned out your advance, which a lot of books never do. You only have to give back your advance if you don't deliver the book. A fabulous advance is a very, very lovely thing.)

On another note, I've had some thoughts about alcohol and drinking. About following the party line as far as quitting is concerned. I think I've become impatient with the cult-like nature of all the quitlit and everyone parroting the same stuff. It feels like entire paragraphs are being repeated in all these different books.

The whole 'everyone who drinks is on the addiction spectrum' line that is so prevalent in most of the quitlit I've read doesn't ring true for me. When you grow up in a huge extended family . . . (Reader, let me intrude to mention that my mother came from a family of ten kids; my dad from a family of eleven. Yes, excellent Catholics. Also, no TV. At one point I had over fifty first cousins) . . . you can very clearly see those who are on the spectrum of alcohol use disorder and those who can take it or leave it. So, I'm afraid I call bullshit on that one.

Also, this idea of 'what's the point of drinking if you can only have one drink on weekends' feels like BS. It could be applied to anything. Sugar is addictive and harmful. What's the point of eating cake if you can only have one piece on weekends?

Life is about control. You have to watch how much junk food you consume; you have to watch how much money you spend; you have to control how much alcohol you drink. That's life.

I may go back to drinking one or two drinks when I go out, but every year I may do one hundred alcohol-free days. I'm going to experiment with various things.

Wednesday
DAY 73

A fucking miracle I'm still off the demon drink considering we're living through a pandemic and an attempted coup.

The one blog I read, I cannot remember which one, said that the weight started dropping off after she reached the two-month mark. Alas, that hasn't been the case for me. My weight as of this morning is 66.9 kg and that's with me practising intermittent fasting and walking two to three times every day. Problem is, with the pandemic and everything happening on Zoom, we are even more sedentary than usual. Good news is that I've managed to keep the weight below my fatty weight of 73.4 that I reached after the first lockdown. But I am craving sugar – probably more than usual – and I do reward myself with a piece of cake every now and again. Seeing that I can't go out for a drink (and with the alcohol ban that's off the cards anyway), I now go out for tea and cake. I'm finding it an excellent substitute.

Friday
DAY 75

Coldest day of the year yesterday and coldest night of the year. Minus four or something. Have to say I have been craving a glass of red wine. But not just any red wine. A really superb glass. Was trying to think of the days I would allow myself to drink:

1. The Firstborn's 21st
2. The combined 21st/18th birthday party (if it happens)
3. The Lastborn's 18th
4. The launch of our Marian book

And what would I limit myself to?

A glass of champagne and a glass of red wine?

Definitely no more than three drinks; anything beyond that and I start feeling wobbly. Then again, I might not drink at all. We shall see.

Vossie's birthday will be around the 100th day of no alcohol, so that would be a good time to break it if I were going to.

Rewarding myself for not drinking alcohol by drinking alcohol. Yes, I know how that sounds.

I'm nervous that if I do have one drink, I'll just forget the whole thing and start drinking again, which I don't want.

Saturday
DAY 76

Our head writer on Show 1 has Covid. No symptoms yet, but it took me five days after the Husband tested positive to show symptoms, and if her little sister is vomiting and man down, then I'm worried about her. She phoned me on Friday because she needed Valoid for her sis. I took them a care package. Am feeling borderline hysterical with worry for her. I'm worried for her as a friend and I'm also worried because of work; I don't know what we'll do without her. We are in the middle of hectic rewrites . . . ugh.

Monday
DAY 78

It's the Husband's birthday today, his second in the pandemic. There's a complete sense of unreality that this thing is still going on. It will probably only be petering out next year – a full two years after it started. We had breakfast at the Service Station in Melville with our BFFs. Being with them made me feel antsy about social occasions without booze. Not that I haven't done it before, but it's going to be hard to stick to. Just keep thinking about the hangovers and the downer the next day.

Oom Cyril spoke last night. Prohibition is over but you can only buy booze from Monday to Thursday and the curfew is still in place. Probably a good thing that we abandoned the surprise 21st birthday party for the Firstborn.

Tuesday
DAY 79

I finished reading *Unbecoming* by Joanne Fedler. The book is about a menopausal woman finding herself and the sense of rage she speaks about, the sense of disconnection from her adult children. I could really relate to that. I often feel like everyone's trying to get at me, whereas I'm pretty sure they're not. I am sick of being taken for granted, but I think any woman of my age with kids probably feels like that. It's also much easier just to let everyone hog the TV, eat all the snacks and treat you like an ATM than it is to actually say something.

Okay, just researched it, and it makes sense that the mood swings can carry on for months. After all, I have been self-medicating with alcohol for 35 years at least. I was already drinking at school, and then at university I started drinking regularly, so, besides when I was pregnant and breastfeeding, I have always been drinking. I wonder if that's why I felt so depressed in the first trimester – because I no longer had booze!

Soooo, mood-wise: I was in a very good mood for a while – obvs the pink cloud effect – now I'm back to the mood swings and the EXTREME anger – totally over the top.

Ho hum.

Let's see how that goes.

Thursday
DAY 81

The Husband cheerily told the owner of Croft & Co this morning that August is the last roll of the dice for him, meaning that after that there is no money in the company. Such a jolly thought. We cannot survive on my salary alone. Made me wish I did something important and lucrative in finance, or in . . . God, I dunno. What do people do that makes loads of lolly?

Although keep imagining having to get out of my pyjamas, put make-up on and brush my hair every day? Not to mention the commuting. Ugh.

Weather is warming up, 19 degrees today. Thanks god.

Going to get my hair blow-dried later for our photo shoot for *Chasing Marian* tomorrow. Woo-hoo!

Weight is still hanging around the just under 67 kg mark. Wore jeans for the first time in about a year yesterday. At least I could fit into them.

I have worn leggings solidly since lockdown began a year and a bit ago; they are starting to lose their elasticity and sort of hang down in the arse area, plus there are holes around the seams.

Super-sexy.

Friday
DAY 82

My blog today was about keeping on keeping on. I wrote about how sometimes it really helps to look back over what you've achieved in your life and see how far you've come.

Keeping on keeping on

I have a tendency to only focus on the things I've failed at (it's true that we only ever remember the bad reviews). I become blasé about things that were really very difficult to achieve.

- When I was living in Maritzburg, the thought of landing an actual acting agent in the big, bad city of Joburg seemed beyond the realms of possibility, but I did it.
- Getting the hang of writing TV scripts seemed *so hard*. I felt like I would never get it right, but I did, and I'm fortunate to still be doing it seventeen years later.
- We started a B&B in 2006, but that, combined with the 2008 crash, got us into so much financial poo that we nearly lost our house. It took us *forever* to get out of that mess.
- I struggled for years to get a novel published: from the time I started writing *Ms Conception* to the time it actually got published was EIGHT YEARS. I am now the published author of three books.

- I thought getting a literary agent was out of my reach. I first tried to get a literary agent in 1998. I finally landed not one, but two literary agents – an international one and a South African one – twenty years later, in 2018.
- I get invited to interview authors for book launches and at literary festivals. Until 2015, I had never been to a book festival and the thought of being on a panel with other authors was beyond terrifying.
- I had my work cut a couple of years ago and honestly did not know how I was going to pay my kids' school fees. I reached out to friends – including young writers I had mentored – and they gave me extra bits of work that got me through. It was a rocky few years, but I am a true freelancer now where I'm not dependent on one project.
- Beyond all of this, the hardest thing I ever did was bring two children into the world. I found the first year of motherhood so tough, I had to write a musical, a stand-up comedy routine and finally a book about it. Thankfully, the children have grown up to be people that I enjoy spending time with.

Yes, things are pretty bleak at the moment, but I have scaled many seemingly insurmountable obstacles in the past and I know I can again.

You can too.

Think about the things you managed to achieve in the past against all odds – particularly if you have been retrenched or are having to close down your business.

Write them all down and remember that you are not worthless. This is about the pandemic, not you.

My last tip when all else fails is to have a good cry. I'm not talking about the pretty shed-a-few-tears-in-a-sad-movie cry. I'm talking about the lying on the bathroom floor, full-on, ugly cry. You will feel a helluva lot better afterwards. Trust me.

And to those who have lost loved ones to Covid, my love and condolences to you all.

ACT II

Okay, maybe one glass . . .

(August 2021 to November 2021)

AUGUST

Sunday
DAY 84

I have a lot of friends born on the 31st of July. It's also the due date of the little baby that never was. The baby I miscarried who, for some reason, we call Henry, would've been 18 yesterday. But as the Firstborn always says, 'Four Leos in the house?! That would've been a bit damn much.' Also, if we'd had Henry, we wouldn't have had our Lastborn.

Yesterday, we were supposed to have the surprise 21st birthday party for the Firstborn at our local, the Blind Tiger. We cancelled it because of Covid; it just felt irresponsible. Most of the family members wouldn't have been able to make it anyway. Just as well we cancelled it. Vossie was horrified at the thought of a surprise party, and he also has a terrible tummy bug, which we are hoping is not Covid. I was just imagining the poor Lastborn trying to drag him to Blind Tiger. It wouldn't have been pretty.

Soooooo, first social outing yesterday since I gave up the tipple. It was the birthday of the twins, Imogen and Iris, and it was the same people whom I'd made a tit of myself in front of on Mother's Day. (Serious question: does anybody actually use the word 'whom' in conversation?) Interesting thing, though, was that some of the others looked a bit sheepish too. I asked Cordelia, the lovely young adult who had been looking after me in my drunken state, what I had been fighting with all the guys about. She thought perhaps they were being sexist. I had been wearing my red wine armour and had taken them on. Anyway, all was smooth and pleasant yesterday.

I drank my dealc'd champers, which was delish, and avoided the shooters – served in syringes, which I just loved! The twins walked around telling everyone to have their vaccination. Those two know how to throw a fabulous party. I went home at 5.30 (pm not am!) so I was there for roughly three hours. As I left, people were starting to get tipsy, but nothing hectic. I did feel a pang of envy as I watched people enjoying a delish glass of red wine. I also noticed, though, the red wine stains around their mouths, and I pictured the hangover I would have had from drinking red wine. I suspect that if I had been drinking, at three hours into the party, I would probably have been a lot drunker than everyone else and talking nonsense. Good thing I stuck to my alcohol-free bubbles.

It was great to meet new people, although admittedly, I did feel slightly out of it as people were discussing their overseas trips and whether to go to Montenegro or Dublin to avoid quarantine, while I was busy worrying about my debit orders bouncing because I will probably only get paid on Wednesday. It's absolutely not their fault; I just felt like I didn't have a lot to contribute to the conversation, so in a way it was a relief to go home, although I did have a little bit of FOMO.

The best part of all this is that I haven't woken up this morning feeling awful, knowing that I have to work or wondering if I did or said anything stupid, and having that awful shame attack followed by the post-party blues.

I was slightly irritated with the Husband because he got home fifteen mins after curfew. Fine if he had been on his own – his problem if he landed up being arrested – but not fine with the Lastborn in the car. Obvs they ubered.

We announced our new book, *Chasing Marian*, on the socials on Friday, leaving Marian out of the equation – we don't want to become those irritating people who tag her in everything (okay, I AM that irritating person). It was so lovely to have something to celebrate in these truly grim times. I also kept watching Tatjana Schoenmaker winning gold at the Olympics for breaststroke on repeat and having a little blub.

I have lost another two colleagues to Covid. Shona Ferguson – I worked with him and his lovely wife on *Rockville* – and Chris Blomkamp, whom I started out with at *Generations*. Both gone. Shona was 47, Chris 44. There is an utter sense of disbelief as this third wave takes its toll.

It's the most glorious day today – dusty blue sky, scent of jasmine in the air – first hint of spring. We need rain.

Thursday
DAY 88

Yesterday was my birthday. I was tempted to have a glass of something, but we went to the Ocean Basket in Melrose for sushi, and the wine there is not exactly anything to write home about, so why drink it? There was an awful, loud woman at the next table who seemed to be performing for everyone.

'SAY THANK YOU!' She kept screeching to her son and 'IN OUR DAY WE DIDN'T HAVE SCREENS TO AMUSE US . . .' Blah, blah, blah. Yes, she had been drinking. Rather a lot, from the sounds of things. Was excited to get the bill and escape her. Melrose was depressing; there are so many empty shops, so many restaurants that have closed down, it left me feeling sad. It's my second birthday in lockdown and I find I have to force myself to celebrate stuff. The only time I feel vaguely normal is when I'm working; everything else feels fairly pointless.

I got my hair and nails done yesterday morning. It did feel good to look pretty, but I'm very impatient and find it hard to relax and wanted to hurry the whole process along.

I am moderating a virtual panel tonight on a non-fiction book dealing with GBV called *When Secrets Become Stories*, edited by fave Sue Nyathi. I'm weirdly nervous and just want to get it over with.

A friend wanted to go out for drinks at Blind Tiger for my birthday on Friday night, but because I'm not drinking, going to the pub feels pointless, so I suggested an early-morning coffee. I do miss the ritual of booze, the feeling of relaxing, and I wonder if that's contributing to my feeling of not wanting to celebrate anything?

I dunno.

Monday
DAY 92

Happy Women's Day!

Not much to be happy about in SA. Rape capital of the world. But I choose to focus on how far we've come. I'm grateful to all the women in my life, grateful that I can vote, and work, and drive, and use birth control, and wear whatever the hell I want.

Spent Saturday watching the rugby at a friend's house. It was the first social occasion I've stayed at until the end. We arrived there after three and left at 9.30 because of the curfew. If there hadn't been a curfew it would've been interesting to see how drunk everyone got because people were already getting merry by then. But I didn't find anyone irritating. I found it quite funny actually and kept wondering about my own behaviour. I'm pretty sure I was waaaaaay more irritating when I was drinking – louder – repeating myself – wanting to love everyone – crying – over-sentimental – all of the above. Ugh. Cringe city.

I also danced, and what hasn't changed is that I still love dancing. My parents were brilliant dancers, I used to love watching them because when they danced, they seemed happy together. I learnt how to jive and rock 'n' roll by dancing with my dad. The older you get, the fewer occasions there are to dance, so I'm always happy to have a reason to get up and jive. We won the rugby and it was a very tense game, so we were literally dancing for joy. There were Springbok shooters to celebrate, made of crème de menthe and Amarula. I missed the fun aspect of that. But after drinking my dealc'd champers, I then moved on to Tab, which I lurrve even though it's so bad for you. Am very pleased they've started making it again. Then I had a cup of tea and a lovely piece of carrot cake, which I really enjoyed. If I had been drinking, I would've been too busy tossing red wine down my throat to be interested in the cake.

Everyone kept commenting on how slim and great I was looking. My weight has not changed so I'm not sure if I look less puffy or they were just trying to console me because I was sober.

When we got home the Husband tucked into ice-cream and the choc peanuts, which were gone the next day, whereas I was so full I didn't want anything else. No post-booze munchies for me (she says, smugly).

I did a lot of thinking back to previous Red Wine Fridays and how, in fact, it was only the first glass of prosecco and perhaps the first glass of red wine that was nice, and then after that I would start feeling horribly drunk, and already have a looming headache. I would take Disprin when I got home, perhaps a sachet of Rehidrat, and then have a terrible night's sleep and feel awful the next day.

NO THANK YOU!

I made the Husband park the car so that I could drive straight out. I hate reversing out of the driveway, not just in case I ding the car, but it also makes me feel vulnerable to hijackers. I need to be facing forward so that I can drive OVER these imaginary hijackers. I also stress that I'll get parked in, and I won't be able to manoeuvre the car out, and that the Husband will argue about leaving and we will break the curfew and then get stopped by the cops and he will get stroppy with them after too much vino and get locked up and be beaten up/raped in jail or perhaps have to defend himself in jail and kill someone else . . .

Did I mention that I write for soapies?

The point of all of this is that I don't have to worry about any of these scenarios with an Uber.

Well, except for it being a fake Uber and the real Uber driver being locked in the boot and—

No. Stoppit.

We did our first radio interview for the book yesterday with the fabulous Sara-Jayne Makwala. It was so exciting. Those are the kinds of things I want to get excited about in the future.

Thursday
DAY 95

I've been thinking a lot about what it takes to create the life you want.

I have now been working in the TV industry for 20 years.

Lawd, how did that happen?

Reader, some background about the life I have had.

I started directing – exceptionally badly – for *Top Billing* in 2001 (a gig organised by a fabulous friend, Tombie Mitchell). When I had been there for a while (still directing badly), I was instructed to go and direct an insert on some celebrity performance of *The Vagina Monologues* that the author, Eve Ensler, was taking part in. The kicker was that they did not want to hear the word 'vagina' (I shit you not). I did a whole bunch of interviews with the celebrity performers and didn't record the actual show (because 'vagina') and got shat upon from a dizzy height as I had no footage of the actual show.

That was my last stint as a director.

Then in 2003 I started writing for my very first show, and I've been writing for TV ever since. It was tough going at first; that first year and a half was a baptism by fire.

After that, I moved to Show 2. That was tough too. Our head writer at the time used to rewrite every single script I handed in, which was very disheartening. Then another head writer took over and I didn't get enough scripts to write.

Once I'd settled into it, it turned out to be a really good run for me. Now it does seem to have come to an end.

We got an email to say that the channel hasn't told them whether or not we're reducing Show 2 to three times a week, but basically that's the money that paid for our food and holidays and put my kids through school, so it was really good.

I'm hoping now to segue into writing dramas and screenplays, and I'll obviously continue writing novels.

I wrote my first attempt at a novel in 1997. At that point you had to post your three chapters to an agent in London, which was unbelievably expensive. I finally got published digitally in 2012. A decade as a published author in 2022.

And yet it is only now, in this year of Our Lord 2021, that I finally receive an advance for a novel. It really does take years and endless perseverance to get the life you want.

And failure.

Soooooooo much failure.

Still, when I look at the jobs other people around me have, it makes me feel very blessed indeed to do something that's so much fun.

Maybe, barring the money issues and the killer virus, I actually do have the life I want.

Sunday
DAY 98

I got my second Covid jab on Friday. About twelve hours later the side-effects started. I was not just shivering but literally shaking, and my teeth were chattering so loudly I thought I would wake the Husband up with the noise. Felt quite shitty yesterday, had the shivers and low-level nausea, but kept downing Panados and then took an Empacod last night to help me sleep because I got no sleep the night before.

Slept beautifully, although felt very zonked this morning. But 48 hours after the jab, I'm definitely feeling a lot better, and my arm is nowhere near as sore as the first time around. The best part is that I'm double-jabbed! Woo-hoo!

I've been watching these Netflix romcoms all weekend, but they've just ended up making me feel completely maudlin because they're about kids going away to college. I've got a year and a half left before my kids go for good and I'm so sad that I haven't been able to give them everything I wanted to give them. And not in terms of things. I'm sad we haven't had money to travel. I hope in the future, we will have.

I also had a moment of sadness that I haven't been able to spend as much time with them as I would've liked. I had to step up to the plate and increase my earnings in 2008 when the Husband's business went to hell in a handbasket due to the economic crisis. Even more so in 2014 after he was retrenched in 2013 and was between jobs for some months. I basically haven't done many school lifts since then.

We joke about it, but I do feel like I've missed out with my kids because I've been working too hard and it's tough when another mother from the school says things like, 'We've seen your Husband at the school, but not you.'

I am finding myself feeling more irritable than usual about our financial situation. We have been in a financial mess since 2008, and with Covid it's just got progressively worse.

Constantly worrying about money is like having a chronic illness. It's very draining.

Wednesday
DAY 101

The Firstborn's 21st birthday today. In honour of his birthday, I will be drinking my first drink in 101 days tonight. It's been three months, and I think it's been long enough to test myself now.

(Reader, background on the birth: on the day I went into labour, I was working like a dog as usual. We had the launch of the Rand Water Project – an educational show we were doing about water awareness, which was a joint venture between Sparrow Schools and my company, Powerhouse Productions. My waters broke in the wee hours of the morning after the launch and after about seventeen hours of labour, the Firstborn swam into the world. Both my kids were born into water, which I highly recommend BTW. I wrote a very thinly disguised autobiographical account of his birth in my first novel, *Ms Conception*.)

Last year, on his 20th birthday, he told us he was gay. He decided to come out then because of Covid. I think there was something about the horror of the pandemic that made everyone want to live a more authentic life. I wrote a blog about it but then got cold feet and didn't publish it. Here is an extract from that unpublished piece:

Living an authentic life

On his 20th birthday, before we did the grand present opening, my son told us that he's gay.

I do have to confess that the Husband did overhear him telling the daughter that he was gay the night before, but as the Husband is deaf, I didn't fully believe it until my son told me the next day. However, it did give me time to quickly google 'What to say when your child tells you he's gay.' Do not say, 'Oh, I always knew.' Or 'It's probably just a phase.' And especially do not say 'You're going to burn in hell.' You could say 'Thank you for telling me.' Or 'I love you no matter what.'

I thought that the son would not want anyone to know after he told us, but he is keen to get the news out there so that he doesn't have to keep announcing it, hence this blog post. I have to admit I was torn about speaking about it here; it feels deeply personal, but the kind of homophobia I've seen on Twitter convinced me that this is an issue that needs to be spoken about and normalised. We also hope that by sharing our experience here, we help other families who are dealing with similar issues. I loathe the fake nature of social media where we talk about all our victories and post pictures of our holidays (even if we hated them) and we don't talk about the stuff that really matters.

Logically, it doesn't make sense that one should have to 'come out' in this day and age. It's not as if you expect your heterosexual children to make a big announcement about their sexual preferences. As the daughter said, no one's waiting for her to say, 'I'm sorry everyone, I like men!' But, of course, we know the world doesn't work like that. It is still a big deal.

After he told us, although it wasn't entirely unexpected, I did feel tearful. I realised it was because I was worried that his life would be more difficult and most of all that people might be mean to him and reject him. That was what concerned me the most. His sister, who is a HUGE fan of RuPaul, has many gay friends and has been attending Pride for years, assured me that she will fight anyone who gives him a hard time.

We celebrated the boy's birthday with a wonderful dinner at one of our favourite restaurants, The Local Grill in Rosebank. As we sat there, he put a message on our extended family group telling everyone the news. My sister rang me immediately. Instead of saying 'Hello', I just said 'Yes. It's true.' My brother-in-law had thought he was bullshitting so she was glad that she had called. The responses on the family group were loving and supportive and set the tone for the evening.

I also let a few of my friends know a couple of days later and once again was overwhelmed by their warmth and support. My one friend told me that if she had to come out, she would want to do it to parents like us, which made me feel reassured.

> ME: *after two glasses of wine* I am going to be the BEST gay mom ever.
> THE SON: I'm sorry, Dad, did Mom never mention she was a lesbian?
> THE DAUGHTER: *massive eyeroll* You're not gay, Mom. He is.

She should be grateful. My mother was astoundingly naïve and used to get bestiality and bisexuality confused, which made for some interesting conversations. *No, Ma. It's not the same thing.*

Thinking back over my son's school experience, I got to thinking about how difficult it must've been for him. He did have the most wonderful head of school in his year (he gave one of the best speeches I have EVER heard at prize-giving), who organised an assembly where kids got to come out and young women got to speak about rape culture, and this year at the school they even flew the pride flag. But still, I doubt there are many schools where it would be permitted to take a same-sex partner to the matric dance or indeed where it would be accepted among the student body. The son said that there was no way on God's green earth he would've felt comfortable taking a boy to the matric dance.

He said that he felt an enormous sense of relief after telling us. He is certainly using it to his advantage, and every time someone asks him to unload the dishwasher or take the massive collection of dirty crockery out of his room his response is either 'Don't be homophobic' or 'I feel oppressed living in this hetero-normative household.' He did ask me if I'm now going to write a book about it and suggested titles like 'The Agony of Having A Gay Son'. My response: yes, 'The Agony of Having A Gay Son Who Has Yet To Learn How To Tidy His Own Room'.

I feel so grateful that he felt able to tell us, that he feels loved and accepted by all of us. He threw the first get-together at our house since prep school for his birthday. His father searched for a pride flag to put up in his bar next to the Springbok and South African ones, but we were unable to find one and had to settle for a rainbow cake instead. If anyone knows where we can get a pride flag, do let us know. Because, yes, we are all very proud of him.

Thursday
DAY 102

So I broke prohibition last night and had a glass of prosecco and a delicious glass of red wine. Did not enjoy the prosecco very much and the Lastborn eventually finished it for me. But the red wine was exquisite. It was a 2016 Boekenhoutskloof Cab Sauv. Soooo yum.

The prosecco went straight to my head but then once I had eaten something I felt fine, and I really enjoyed the wine. Although the combo of red meat and red wine did mean I had insomnia in the wee hours. The food was absolutely exquisite, though, and it was a good evening. I had felt nervous about having a glass of wine, like perhaps I would immediately break into their wine cellar and start consuming everything in sight. Luckily, I didn't as that would've been an expensive exercise at Marble.

I have to admit that the beginning of yesterday was not so great. I woke up with a migraine. I think I was feeling very sad about my firstborn turning 21. Possibly it was a reaction to the jab – I seem to remember having something similar the first time around. I was feeling robbed of all the excitement that celebration brought before the pandemic made its grand entrance. I was also feeling panicky, like we are running out of time to have experiences as a family. I suspect this could be the beginning of empty-nest syndrome. You've devoted your life to your kids, now what? I was feeling very weepy the whole morning but luckily, the fab four cheered me up with their silliness (our *Chasing Marian* WhatsApp group is the funniest thing evah!) and my headache receded, and I got a whole lot of work done and even dressed up for our night out.

The best part was getting home and finding the homemade card for my son from Beatrice and her daughter, together with two hundred rand. I found that so unbearably moving, I wanted to blub all over again.

Sunday
DAY 105

I found out on Friday that Karen, the mother of the daughter's best friend from prep school, passed away, from non-Covid pneumonia. They live around the corner from us. Husband and wife seemed to do everything together. I can't get it out of my mind because it selfishly made me think of the Husband and me, and how bereft we would be without each other. Also, with Covid, we are being confronted by our mortality daily and we are just not used to it.

Simultaneously, there is this seize-the-day feeling but we are restricted from seizing the day by various lockdown regulations and by the general wretchedness everyone is feeling. It's difficult to enjoy stuff when people are sick/dying/going through unimaginable hardships.

We went to watch a movie at Hyde Park yesterday. Husband had a glass of wine. I had a cappuccino. He said the wine tasted like paint stripper, so I was glad to be sober curious. It was lovely to get out. It's easy to just sink into the couch in front of Netflix every weekend, especially when everything is so gloomy, you have to force yourself to do stuff. The vaccinations opened to the 18 to 34-year-olds at midnight on Thursday and they are coming out in their droves. The Firstborn has a driver's test on Thursday and so will wait until after that. Lastborn is very jealous not to be eligible for the vaccines.

I am busy sorting out grown-up stuff – not my favourite thing. I've been gathering everything together to renew my driver's licence on Tuesday. I have to pay someone a small fortune to jump the queue and drive all the way to Krugersdorp for the privilege, because I couldn't get an appointment at Randburg. Which, after watching the doccie *Devilsdorp*, about those Satanic murders in Krugersdorp, freaks me out slightly. I also went to the dermatologist on Friday. It was the first time the Husband had ever been and unfortunately the doc told him what beautiful skin he has, and he hasn't stopped boasting about it ever since. Eye tests this week – I literally cannot drive at night – and in September teeth cleaning. I then have to fit in the pap smear, boob exam and, joy of joys, a colonoscopy at some point.

This is another thing you can put out of your mind when you're on the booze. All these thoughts of the health checks you should be having just float right out of your mind when you have a few glasses of wine. You can make time to go to the pub and you can spend money on pricey wines, but not on your health. It's nuts.

Work is beyond crazy, and my back is creaking in protest. I have a script to write today for the one show – the deadline is tomorrow morning – and three scripts to finish editing for the other show. I am so grateful for the work. Obvs the money is of paramount importance with the business is in the doldrums, BUT I'm also so happy to be busy, for my mind to be occupied. It's a terrible time to be alone with your thoughts for too long.

Monday
DAY 106

The Husband called me over and said 'before you go inside, blow this'.

No. Not that. Take your mind out of the gutter.

It was a dandelion.

'Make a wish,' he said. So I did.

I wished that this shitshow would be over.

We saw mothers from Roo's school at the coffee shop. One thing I hate about the kids being at school is that you feel you're at school too. There is this subtle and not-so-subtle competition about everything. Where everyone's going on holiday (um . . . nowhere for us). How far kids are in terms of learning how to drive. It's couched in 'Oh my god, my child is such a dreadful driver.' But it's really just humble-bragging and being competitive. Also, the one mother said, 'So, I heard Roo's given up swimming?' with so much relish, I did want to slap her. Hard.

When I got back home, I vented to the Lastborn about it.

Response from Lastborn? 'Some parents don't have anything else in their lives, Ma. That's why they have to live through their kids.'

Then I felt mean for complaining. Because, although we may be in financial shit, the Husband and I are so lucky to have each other, and the kids are so lucky to have a secure, loving home. Plus, my family are forever just giving me things. We are surrounded by gifts from them. So much furniture, including a piano from Big Brother and family, the computer my two brothers and nephew built for the son, the little car my sister gave the kids, the expensive iPad my brother-in-law gave the daughter to do her art. We go on fantastic holidays courtesy of Maudie and her man. I'm the laatlammetjie. I'm always trying to catch up and I wish I could do nice things for everyone else.

I read that story about George Clooney calling his friends together – the ones who had really stood by him – and giving each of them a million dollars in a suitcase. I won't be quite that extravagant. Mine will be a million rand and it will just be a bank transfer.

One day . . .

Last night, after I got through my insane workload (I basically wrote and delivered a script in five hours after I finished my other work), I was craving a glass of red wine. But I thought beyond the first sip to the wine making me feel a bit pissed, followed by talking nonsense, not having a great sleep, and then waking up with a bit of a headache, and suddenly I didn't feel like a glass after all.

There was thunder and about five drops of rain last night.

More unrest is predicted for tomorrow. *Sigh*

Onwards and upwards.

Tuesday
DAY 107

Today I went off to Devilsdorp and paid six hundred and fifty ronts to a character called Ricky to renew my licence. I felt proud of myself driving there as it's almost an hour away and thankfully not on the freeway. I could travel at a sedate 80 kays the whole way. I had no idea where to park and ended up parking in the spot reserved for those taking their truck licences. Someone very kindly came and told me to move.

I was exhausted when I got back but very pleased with myself for my adulting 101.

We needed to buy some asparagus for dinner so we popped into our local for a drink. The Husband had a couple of beers while I had Earl Grey tea and dessert. I couldn't be bothered to just sit there while he drank, which is why I ordered something to eat. Have to confess that I did feel a bit ill after the pud and have decided that eating sweet things at pubs is not the answer, because I will weigh 150 kg at the end of this if I do.

What is the answer? No fucking idea. I'm leaving booze behind but I don't have anything to replace it with yet.

I love the ritual of opening a bottle of wine. I love meeting friends at the pub. I love the feeling of being slightly tipsy. These can't be replaced with anything else. You have to accept that.

When you're on the outside looking in, though, this is what you notice:

- ✔ People talk at you, not to you
- ✔ People are argumentative
- ✔ Suddenly things like reckless driving are funny
- ✔ Wine breath is not good
- ✔ Red wine stains on your mouth are not pretty
- ✔ The sloppiness of it all.

It's not sexy. And when you are watching all of this, it's really not funny at all.

I remember in 2009 when Mom was recovering from her bowel resection after being diagnosed with bowel cancer and could no longer drink alcohol, a cousin who used to be a great drinking buddy of hers was supposed to come around and visit her when Mom was staying at ours. We waited all afternoon and were eventually given some bullshit excuse that she couldn't find the house. The truth of the matter was that she was no longer interested in visiting because there was no booze on offer.

What made me think of this?

It's Evie's birthday today. She would've been 85.

Friday
DAY 110

It was Karen's memorial service today. On Zoom. Actually on Teams – but same-same. I found it unbearably sad. I was trying to find pictures of her to send to her husband and what I found was a picture of my book *Things Unseen* with a little comment from Karen saying, 'Waiting for an autograph'. How kind she was to always support my work. Kindness is becoming more and more important to me.

This makes me think of how arrogant I used to be. I thought I was somehow special because I'd had some books published, that I was this kind of celeb. Alcohol made me constantly feel like I wasn't good enough as I am, but at the same time it filled me with this kind of grandiose self-importance.

We've had such a rough last decade – personally and as a country –

that I realise now that all this stuff I surround myself with is a veneer. It could be taken away at any second. The trouble in KZN just confirmed that.

Embarking on this sober curious journey has made me realise what a dick I have been. Perhaps I never said things to people's faces, but I certainly thought them and would've made a snide comment to my nearest and dearest. I always prided myself on my compassion – but it only really extended to the 'cool' group of friends I surrounded myself with. Being funny was always more important to me than being kind.

I'm not about to become a massive bore, but I definitely do not want to go back to the person that I was. I feel ashamed of some of the shit I said and did. And how I flirted with men I frankly wasn't even interested in – I just needed them to be interested in me.

(Note to self: Daddy is never going to love you, stop trying so hard. Also, you're not actually that sexy. Get over yourself.)

On the Covid front: looks like the third wave will just roll into the fourth wave. How lovely.

Sunday
DAY 112

Freezing weather from yesterday afternoon. Sheet of ice inside the fountain at 11 o'clock.

Bruce Young wrote a very interesting blog about climate change and how things are not quite as simple as we think they are and that changing over from petrol and chemicals is not going to happen with a snap of our fingers. He speaks about all the mass extinctions there have been and that we think we're a lot more important to the earth than we actually are. Piles of garbage everywhere. Polluted water and air. Global warming will lead to even more fires, floods and heatwaves.

But are people really about to stop flying?

I doubt it. Things are not that simple. If I look back, my embracing of homeopathy and natural remedies was really quite extreme. Breastfeeding even though I was in excruciating pain, for instance. Or having a shit fit because the Moms and Tots teacher gave the kids NikNaks.

Hilarious! Especially because both kids promptly got asthma despite all the water births and breastfeeding and organic food and no antibiotics.

Life is so much more complicated than we think it is.

The same applies to the whole booze issue. Everyone is not going to immediately quit drinking. The world is not suddenly going to become booze-free.

To be honest, I think moderation is key. I'm never going to give up drinking completely, but I certainly don't want to go back to drinking like I was. I hope I can give myself a weekly or monthly limit and stick to it.

I am shallow enough to want Jennifer Lopez's fabulous skin, which is apparently achieved through not drinking, but also to want to have the odd glass of red wine. Let's see if I'll be able to have my cake and eat it – and make trifle out of it too.

Tuesday
DAY 114

Last day of winter, hurrah!

Yes, yes, thank you, Twitter know-it-alls, for telling me that meteorological spring only begins on the 21st of September.

Spring blossoms are out. Gorgeous peach, wild pear and cherry blossoms. There are acid-green leaves on the plane trees by the park. The hope of spring is in contrast to the limping exhaustion of this pandemic. The scientists have discovered some new Covid variant and, honestly, I wish they'd just fuck off with their new variants. I am sooooooo tired of this pandemic and of the general feeling of hopelessness. I have to frantically juggle money towards the end of the month because we only get paid on the fourth. Poor old school fees get paid late because of it, but I think a lot of peeps aren't paying their fees at all, so they're probably grateful for my contribution at this point.

Passed cousin Michael on my walk this morning. (Reader, my publisher reminded me that it's not name-dropping if you don't drop a name, so I'm duty-bound to share that my cousin is the renowned actor,Michael Richard.) He complimented me on my sober curious blog post. He referred to it as a podcast, which confused me slightly. I told him that the boozing had been getting a bit out of hand, which was why I had needed to calm the fuck down.

The Firstborn got his driver's licence yesterday on his second attempt after I forked out a VAST sum of cash for it. Not in bribes, in driving lessons. His driving instructor was an anti-vaxxer Christian fundamentalist, and the examiner was a bizarre Idi Amin-type figure, who spoke on the phone constantly throughout and yelled at the Firstborn telling him he'd failed. But in the end he passed.

Only in Devilsdorp.

I am excessively glad we do not have to make any more trips to Devilsdorp. Well, not until it's the Lastborn's turn. She has just got her learner's, so the whole painful process starts over again. The Husband is the one who teaches them, I don't have the stomach for it, I just fork out for lessons and feel the pain in my pocket.

One good piece of news: Firstborn is planning on getting vaccinated today!

Thought this morning: what is the meaning of life?

- To love and be loved.
- To do work that you enjoy.
- To find moments of joy.
- To try and be a reasonable human being.
- To leave the world a better place.

Not much else matters.

SEPTEMBER

Wednesday
DAY 115

Happy spring day!

It's 26 degrees in Joburg, the wisteria is just starting to come out, the jasmine is glorious and the leaves on the poor shothole-borer-infected oak are sprouting. We also just received the money from that German company called Enpact that has given us a grant to get back on our feet, which is very good news. Money had to be paid into our personal account, so I told the Husband he's only getting mine once I've been paid.

The Firstborn (who is now vaccinated!) has been doing lifts for us but inquired this morning if he couldn't be paid for it. Typical Joburg hustler. We told him his payment would be that he would be allowed to live in the house. We were only half-kidding.

I was wondering after I had that glass of wine and prosecco at his 21st birthday dinner if I wouldn't start to have the teensiest craving for booze. And yes, yes, I did. I think it has to do with the weather warming up and it being downhill to Christmas from here. When something nice happens, I think, 'Oooooh! Let's have a glass of champers.' And then I feel sort of deflated at the thought that I can't have champers.

Going out for a drink was always a cheap and easy source of entertainment.

I am booked to get my nails done on Sunday with some mates – supposedly we are drinking bubbles while having our manis and pedis. It's at 11 in the morning, so I'll drink coffee. I could also take dealc'd bubbles but not sure I could be bothered. Seems an unnecessary expense.

I do actually like the idea of never drinking again. I like the idea of being this healthy creature with beautiful skin and a calm demeanour who runs marathons—

Steady on, old girl. More like runs five kays.

But you get my drift? I would absolutely *love* to get to the point where booze is a nonentity in my life. I think what the decider for me will be is if my cholesterol has dropped because of being booze-free. If it's risen, then I'll know that I should be drinking a little bit of vino to thin my blood.

Yes, yes, alright, there is a part of me that's hoping that the nurse says, 'Look at that cholesterol! Let's administer red wine immediately!'

Thursday
DAY 116

I think I've been trying to find a way out of this whole never-drinking-again experiment. It's kind of too enormous to consider it on that scale.

Yet, when I ask myself if my life is better without booze, it is. Immeasurably.

Pros:

- ✔ No more hangovers
- ✔ No more insomnia
- ✔ Fewer headaches
- ✔ No more popping Disprin
- ✔ No more embarrassing behaviour
- ✔ No more shame attacks
- ✔ Saving money
- ✔ Better skin
- ✔ Better health.

Cons:

- ✔ No more red wine
- ✔ No more bubbles
- ✔ No more wine/champers tasting
- ✔ No more going to the pub
- ✔ No more silly behaviour when you've had a few
- ✔ FOMO
- ✔ Holidays won't be the same
- ✔ Social gatherings won't be the same
- ✔ Being on a different wavelength to friends, family – the drinking culture
- ✔ The end of some friendships
- ✔ Not fitting in
- ✔ Driving!

Okay, the cons list is longer than the pros list – #worrying.

Still, I suspect I'm just going to have to find the courage inside myself to BE different, to hold myself to a higher standard – without being all horribly judgie about people who drink. Because my worry is that as soon as I have one glass, that will be it. That I will just end up drinking all the time and be back where I started.

I have also had the realisation that I actually do not need to participate in boozy outings. I don't need to go to the rugby. I don't have to go to the pub.

The Husband can still do those things, I don't have to.

I mean I want to, but I don't have to.

Saturday
DAY 118

We were invited to Blind Tiger last night, but I wasn't keen and the Husband wasn't either because he'd already been out the night before. Really enjoyed my evening in – chatting to the kids and watching Netflix with the Husband. I was reminded of how wonderful it is to be booze-free.

My eczema has gone and so has the pain in my gall bladder. Health-wise I feel so much better and over weekends, I'm so . . . happy! Booze is such a downer. I might love getting off my face and adore the taste of red wine, but it's totally not worth it. Life is better with no booze. I absolutely hate to have to admit that but it's true.

I just feel so much more content and so much more able to live in the moment.

Sunday
DAY 119

Just had my nails done at house of new friend, Cressida. She was the year above me at drama school. A thoroughly lovely person, so awesome of Iris to organise it. We chatted about the fact that I've given up booze. Iris has a lot of the fears I have – about being out of sync with everyone else when you quit. The girls were all getting mildly tipsy on mimosas, which I didn't envy as much as I thought I would.

Chatting with Cressida reminded me of my drama school escapades. How I got so drunk with some drama friends at someone's digs that I ended up first taking a bath with this guy I had been flirting with and then shagged him on my friend's bed (in? on? Whatevs, you get the gist).

Met the Husband the following year and then found out that he and my one-night stand were friends. They're still friends on Facebook, which the Husband is unfazed by but which I find super-cringey.

Plus, the friend whose bed I used turned up as the head of the PTA at the son's school. I was so flustered when I saw her again, I agreed to serve on the PTA. Two and half years of penance. Arghhhhhhhh!

Monday
DAY 120

Four months of no booze and I do feel pretty wonderful and maybe the teensiest bit smug, which is less attractive. So great to wake up on a Monday morning and not feel vaguely headachy and liverish and to know that I didn't say anything stupid – well, no more stupid than I would sober.

Yesterday, I was the one who was trying to listen, to have authentic convos with the girls. I wasn't being loud and outrageous. Okay, I did mention the thing about shagging the one-night stand in the friend's bed – but because I said it when I was sober, I didn't feel any remorse. I also spoke about menopause and how I feel on a much more even keel emotionally. And a bit like a man – I certainly have almost as much facial hair as a man. People moan about menopause, but I love it. Besides the facial hair, of course. No more PMT, horrible period pains, bleeding like a stuck pig – I feel kick-ass and powerful. Does that have do with not having men all over you anymore, constantly feeling like someone's prey? It's a relief to no longer be viewed as a piece of meat. And let's be honest, as a piece of meat, one was always wanting in some aspect or another; it didn't matter how fabulous you were looking.

I was mourning the loss of booze, but I'm starting to see a very faint glimmer at the end of the tunnel. Like maybe, just maybe, my life without booze might actually be better.

Iris felt awful that she had given me a bottle of Moët for my birthday. I told her a bottle of Moët is *never* wasted. The kids have been licking their lips and eying it. How did I produce kids that feel like they should only drink French Champagne?!

The great thing about me not drinking is that I have also curbed the kids' drinking. There just isn't really any liquor around the house and I don't automatically offer them a glass of prosecco or champers or a gin.

And maybe a lot of their not drinking might be about example. If they see that I can live a really great life without booze, they will feel that they can too.

Well, that's the theory.

Tuesday
DAY 121

Back to school today. The Lastborn had swimming at 6 am, poor thing. First proper thunderstorm of the season last night but not very much rain. At least it sorted out the dust in the air. Maybe I won't be sneezing as much.

I was battling the all-or-nothing idea of giving up drinking, but I suspect there may be no half-measures for me. That by having that glass of wine, I will just set up the craving for it again.

I keep hanging on to what I've read in more than one book about remembering going to parties when we were kids. We didn't drink, and the parties were exciting and magical, and we still had a whole bunch of fun. I would love to get back to that state where I can have the most fun without booze. Where I don't need it anymore. Where not drinking is normal. I look forward to that day. I'm already loving the fact that I just feel so much happier. Even with the Go See Do business in the toilet and having to edit 90 scripts by the end of November and our novel by mid-October.

Eeek.

I am putting the finishing touches to the screenplay I'm submitting for the Final Draft Competition towards the end of September. It's a screenplay based on the life of the former head of the PAC, Letlapa Mphahlele.

Letlapa was the head of APLA during apartheid and ordered the St James Church and the Heidelberg Tavern attacks. (Reader, in case you're very young, or have forgotten, PAC stands for the Pan Africanist Congress, and APLA stands for Azanian People's Liberation Army. APLA was the PAC's military wing.)

The mother of one of the victims of the Heidelberg Tavern attack, Ginn Fourie, confronted Letlapa at his book launch many years later. This led to them going on a journey of forgiveness. Together they started the Lyndi Fourie Foundation. It's the most amazing story and I would so love for it to get made. We started working on it two years ago in August 2019. In screenplay terms, two years is nothing.

A quarter of adults in SA are now vaxxed. But it's still too slow. There's talk of them lifting the Level 3 restrictions this week. Gauteng is over the third wave, but more people need to get vaxxed before the fourth wave hits around November or December.

PS: I have decided to start keeping a food and exercise diary. As with money, as soon as I don't keep track, things get out of control. The secret to living a good life for me is to be disciplined. Might not work for everyone else. Does work for me. Just before I gave up booze in May my weight was 67.1. This morning it was 68.3. I need to stop eating every bit of sugar I can lay my hands on, and I need to add weights to my walking. I'm not worried about my weight per se, but I do feel flabby. I want to firm up.

Wednesday
DAY 122

Happy. That's how I'm feeling. I really have no business being content with everything being so uncertain, but I am, and I can only attribute it to giving up booze. Not putting a known depressant into my body every night is making me feel great. All I know is that I don't want to lose this feeling.

Thursday
DAY 123

So much for that.

The happy mood did not last and I'm feeling wide-eyed with sheer horror today at the financial mess we are in. The only light I see at the end of the tunnel is the light of an oncoming train. And the thing about being off the booze is that I can't pop off to the pub and self-medicate. I have to feel these feelings.

Everybody's been expecting stuff from me this morning. I have spent five hours on crap that has nothing to do with my job and I'm feeling a leetle pissed-off about it. I'm often unsure whether feelings are justified or not. A friend I haven't seen in a while kept messaging me asking me for shit while I was in the middle of a hectic deadline and also while I was busy doing stuff that had absolutely nothing to do with my bloody job, so my messages to her got more and more terse.

Do I have any right to be irritated by her? I ended up feeling guilty for it, but those are my feelings. It's complicated and bound up in the fact that she is very kind, so I feel beholden. But I don't want to do things because I feel beholden but because I want to.

Also, apologising for something being a pain in the ass doesn't make it any less of a pain in the ass. She doesn't get how hectic my job is. A lot of people don't. They think, 'Ah writing, how lovely! I'm sure she's got time to come out for lunch/be head of the PTA/read my daughter's novel.'

No, I really, really don't have time. Grrrrrrr.

Friday
DAY 124

Remember when I said I was feeling jittery and wanting to drink less coffee? Now I want to drink more. I want, like, ALL the coffee. If I could take it intravenously, I would. Might need to do a caffeine detox at some point. Is it the caffeine making me irritable or am I just justifiably irritated at my ridiculous workload?

Those 90 scripts we're supposed to get out by the end of November? It's never going to happen.

I bend over backwards to fulfil these crazy deadlines, where I've just got to accept that they're just not doable. The work is what suffers if we try and rush the process.

Sunday
126 DAYS

Finished reading *Sober is the New Black* (by Rachel Black – geddit?). Again, this chick had the kind of cravings I couldn't relate to. Drinking close to a bottle of wine a day. However, I came across some research that said that people with alcohol use disorder have this thing where alcohol releases more dopamine than in normal peeps. That they feel more drunk after their first glass.

Me, me and me.

I can feel completely tanked after one glass *and* I also drink too fast. I just don't seem to be able to metabolise alcohol like other people can. I still disagree that booze tastes shit. In a number of the books I've read, they go on and on about how shit booze tastes. I adore the taste of a really lovely glass of red.

What I adore more is the contentment I feel now. I also adore not spending the weekend feeling vaguely hungover.

And yes, I could completely have a glass of red wine and not drink the whole bottle, but it's a slippery slope. If I have one glass, it'll be a hop and a skip until I'm drinking every night again. I know this. And it's not just me. It's the pressure. We live in a society awash with social inebriation.

Easier for the moment just to be abstinent.

We were invited to Red Wine Friday, but we said no. Work. I would be lying if I said I didn't feel a pang for the days when we used to pop down the road for Red Wine Friday. It was so much fun, the kids swimming in the pool and getting up to mischief. But I also remember the horrible hangovers.

We once decided to do Bikram yoga the day after a Red Wine Friday session. We'd never done it before, and I had a moderate hangover. Nor had I slept because I was nervous about what the yoga was going to involve. Luckily, Meg (Megan Thomas is the daughter of a friend and she is a fabulous writer) came along with us because she also wanted to try it. Thanks god she felt faint and had to have a little lie-down because it meant I could abandon the locust pose and look after her. Frankly, if she hadn't, I would've licked the sweat off the scantily clad man in front of me, I was so dehydrated.

Things like that are not fun at the time but they do make a great story.

Tuesday
DAY 128

Been feeling very anxious and overwhelmed lately. We're on this crazy schedule and people are not handing stuff in on time. Wondered why I was feeling so stressed and then I realised that I used to medicate with that glass of wine every night. Coffee in the morning to wake me up and wine at night to calm me down and help me to forget about my awful work deadlines. Was wracking my brain to think of how I should calm myself and then the penny dropped – I shouldn't be working like this.

I should not be working like this.

Wine was helping to keep me on this treadmill. I work too hard. The issue is not me, it's the work. It's just another one of my addictions.

Sunday
DAY 132

We won most outstanding writing team at an Award Show for Show 1. Incredible. Show 3 was also nominated so it was an embarrassment of riches. I did reflect on the fact that young writers see us celebrating the award and think that that's what TV writing is about. Yet here I sit in my holey leggings and ancient, baggy jersey, no make-up and unbrushed hair, working furiously on a Sunday. THAT is what writing is about. Particularly TV writing. And if you want to produce excellent work, you have to put in the hours.

I had pizzas with Ophelia on Friday night. She got pissed on two large glasses of wine, she was slurring, and her eyes were unfocused. I didn't judge her. I judged me – that's exactly what I must look like after drinking. It wasn't a pleasant realisation.

We also went to Shiv's for brunch on Sunday where prosecco was on offer.

Vossie enjoyed a few glasses of fizz and when we got home was about to drive the daughter down to the shops when I stopped him and told him he couldn't because he'd been drinking. If I'd been pissed on prosecco, would I have stopped him? Possibly not.

Alcohol makes all the edges fuzzy, makes me feel like nothing matters, that we can all just relax, everything will be fine.

Even driving under the influence.

Tuesday
DAY 134

There is a real sense that things are opening up here in SA. The anti-vaxxers are still going nuts: there was a crazy march of mainly white people at Sea Point in Cape Town over the weekend. (Why do white people always look so ridiculous at protests? We should just stand and hold placards.) Personally, I don't think we should fight with people. They should just be excluded if they're not vaxxed – exactly as kids are excluded from schools if they are not vaccinated.

I am not scared anymore. I've had the beta variant and am a #doubled vaxxedkween. If I get it, it will be like the flu. I'll also take the top-up jab next year if I have to.

Have started reading *Sunshine Warm Sober,* which is Catherine Gray's riff on stone cold sober. I guess my mind is gradually coming around to the idea of never drinking again. I still take the odd sip of the Husband's red wine, and it's weird. It's as if that taste is enough and then I carry on drinking my Tab. Am loving the idea of the fabulous skin I will have from not drinking. Maybe that's the title of the memoir. 'Vanity made me quit.' Catchy, no?

Wednesday,
DAY 135

My father's birthday today. He would've been 98. Also, the first day of spring, astrologically speaking. A rather chilly day for that. We still haven't had a decent thunderstorm.

Am getting into *Sunshine Warm Sober*. She speaks about how alcohol is everywhere, and we are constantly pushed to drink. On cards, in memes, at gyms, at yoga, everywhere. But we don't even bat an eyelid, even though what's been promoted is essentially a drug.

The Firstborn was caught on his first foray into dope smoking at school and was sent to an addiction counsellor and given a final warning. Just by the bye, the addiction counsellor took him through all the drugs and how they are taken, so that he knew more about drugs than when he went in there. But from this little episode, one of his friends was expelled. The hypocrisy is overwhelming because alcohol is considered absolutely A-okay. I mean, perhaps you can't haul out your hip flask in double maths, but I did hear the deputy head make a joke about all the boys being hungover on a Monday.

I say this not to point fingers because I thought exactly the same. Alcohol was fine, drugs were bad. The bit I didn't get is that alcohol is a drug. A drug that made my childhood pretty miserable due to my mother's addiction. (BTW, I am telling this story with the Firstborn's permission.)

Friday
DAY 137

Heritage Day. What white South Africans should be wearing on this day is still one of life's little mysteries.

Slightly good news on the work front – we might have a second season of Show 1. So that's something. I have decided to not write blogs for the next two months at least. I'm hopelessly overstretched workwise. I wrote two scripts on Show 3 on top of everything else in the last two days. Next week I have to get eight scripts out by Friday, plus I'm doing an author interview on Tuesday, and I will no doubt also have one or two scripts to write. And I'm not sure when we'll have to start editing *Chasing Marian,* but that will be soon. It's crazy.

I'm toying with the idea of taking a social media break. I want to focus on my work, and social media – particularly the anti-vaxxer stuff, and from people I used to respect – is hard to take.

I'm kind of learning to respect myself a bit more, not feeling like I've got to constantly please people, rescue them, save them – do my Christian duty – a message drummed into me from the moment I was born. 'Pick up your cross' was the refrain of my childhood. I am starting to realise that, no, I do not have to carry a cross for the sake of it.

Plenty of shitty things – like global pandemics – happen in life without us finding extra crosses to pick up and carry. Contentment is what I'm after.

Putting on my own oxygen mask before helping anyone else.

Sunday
DAY 139

Besides *Chasing Marian,* this is the first time in a long time I haven't been working on a novel in my spare time. Spare time? Me? Hilarious!

(Reader, I have been trying to crack the international market for years now, and came very close to that elusive fabulous overseas deal in 2018. I really thought it was going to be my year. My second book, *Things Unseen,* was optioned for TV – which means a company dishes out some cash to secure the rights to make a show out of it – and I got a fabulous international agent who told me I was going to be one of the leading titles at the Frankfurt Book Fair and my book was going to be an amazing success. And she had a 100 per cent hit rate so I couldn't fail.

Guess what?

I spoilt her 100 per cent hit rate. The book did not sell, and she and I eventually parted ways. It was for the best really. Some things just aren't meant to last.)

The message I've been getting is to appreciate what I have and work with what I've got. I'm tired of trying to get published overseas and I want to focus on the books set here. From the moment we moved here from Zim in 1984, I fell in love with the place. After suburban Harare, I thought Yeoville was the coolest place on earth. I know everyone thinks we're crazy not to live in Cape Town, but I adore Joburg.

Monday
DAY 140

I've been reading about friendship and sobriety. The sad thing is that one has to embrace the fact that some friendships won't survive abstinence because they were based on bonds of various stages of drunkenness. True friendship, though, will endure.

I'm hoping my temperance is making me a more attentive and present parent. I think a lot of the time I felt impatient with the kids and wanted to bugger off to the pub. I hope I'm more there for them because their happiness matters so much to me.

I get angry with my parents for not putting my happiness first in the decisions they made. But when we know better, we do better. My kids didn't ask to be born, so I have to step up to the plate and try and give them the best childhood and education that I can possibly give them.

Thursday
DAY 143

I am rereading *Sober Curious* by Ruby Warrington. These books are so unbelievably useful. I know exactly what she means about the sheer joy one feels when you give up booze. You don't realise that you've been numbing yourself all this time. The numbing definitely helps you through the difficult times – now that work is so damn hectic, I crave a glass of red wine at night. But the price for that is the downer afterwards. Or not even a downer, you just don't feel the joys as intensely. Honestly, I get quite transported by the scent of the syringa blossoms these days. Pretty much like a cat with catnip!

First proper storm of the season last night and the smell of that rain took me back to Christmas in Zimbabwe as a kid. I felt a huge wave of nostalgia.

Business is terrible for the poor Husband and bloody people are refusing to get vaxxed, which just means that the fourth wave in December will be hectic. I have a little bit of cash set aside that I offered to give him but he's not keen to take it as he says I'll probably never get it back and it's money I'm saving for Christmas/holidays/Lastborn's birthday/her matric dance.

Some lovely news. Youngest nephew Scottie, true to his name, got engaged to a gorgeous Scots lass. I told him that I'm off the grog. I will give myself permission to drink at his wedding, though. If I wish to, that is.

I like Ruby Warrington's take on this, about allowing yourself to drink and not getting caught up in perfectionism. Because I wasn't physically addicted to booze, I can take it or leave it. The trick, though, is that you cannot then fall into drinking every week, otherwise the purpose has been defeated.

Did a virtual book launch on Tuesday night for Qarnita's fabulous, fabulous *Being Dianne*. Usually, I would've been downing the wine during it. This time I was Sunshine Warm Sober and just as well, as Q's internet went down halfway through, and I had to improvise for a good few minutes. Schim and Amy H popped up at the end of the interview as a surprise to Q and it really was rather lovely. I was hoping to not experience the crash after. My mood always plummets after these events. Alas. Being sober means feeling things more deeply, so I felt the crash more deeply too. Also, have had a headache this whole week.

And so much for not writing blogs and getting off social media. I've decided to keep on with them, taking it one day at a time. If I get to the point where I really don't have time, I will quit.

I have to keep reminding myself to stop killing myself for other people. I am a complete doormat with WELCOME written on my forehead. It's not their fault I do, it's mine, and only I can stop it.

Go See Do is our business so it's not ideal me not writing blogs. True, I don't get paid for it, but we really want the business to take off, and if I stop writing for them, it's like I'm giving up. The optics are not good.

Around 22 per cent of adults in SA are fully vaxxed.

OCTOBER

Sunday
DAY 146

We went to Shiv's yesterday, which is miiiiiiiles away from us. She has been renovating in the hopes of turning some of the rooms into spaces she could rent out on Airbnb. The place is looking fantastic. We had a lovely day, but I felt as nervous as hell driving back from her place as the designated driver. I asked Maudie and the Husband in the back of the car just to help remind me of the turn-off I needed to take, but as strong drink had been imbibed, they were unhelpful. Then the Husband thought he'd have a bit of fun at my expense.

> HUSBAND: How many times have you been out here?
> ME: Doesn't matter. I battle to see at night.
> HUSBAND: But you've got new glasses so really there's no excuse.
> ME: *screeches to a halt* Would you like to get out and walk?
> HUSBAND: . . .
> SISTER: *babbles nervously*

I was not amused. Realisation: being the designated driver and having to drive at night is scary, but what is freaking me out much more than that is being sober around drunk people. And especially the drunk people closest to me. It triggers me because it reminds me of my mother, and I start getting all dog's-bum-mouthed and judgie.

But then I think, who the actual fuckitty-fuck do you think you are, thinking like that, you binge-drinking soak, you sanctimonious, farty-broek, suddenly-sober person??

('Suddenly Sober' – good book title.)

And then I feel a huge wave of shame at all the times I pressed people to drink more and made fun of them for not getting into the party mood like the rest of us. I guess I am reaping what I sowed now.

If you stand back and remove the emotion from it, the pure fact of the matter is that you are just on a different plane to everyone else when you're not drinking. I feel like I'm in Paris and I'm stuck with my appalling schoolgirl French and people are laughing at me and mocking me for my pronunciation (that really did happen). Drunk peeps have a mean edge. And they definitely speak a different language to the sober.

Some good news is that someone phoned the Husband and asked him to send a CV for a six-month stint in Pretoria. Yes, it will be hectic for me with lifts and everything but what bliss for him to get a salary every month.

The Lastborn was made Head of House and Head of Swimming. Am so chuffed for her.

The Firstborn is stressed about exams and is having a bit of a crisis about what he wants to do with his life.

Has been pissing with rain. So much so that the one rose bush keeled over. Think we're supposed to have a rainy summer. Not again. Ugh.

Tuesday
DAY 148

The Husband has an interview tomorrow afternoon with these peeps, but I'm feeling too cynical and jaded to get my hopes up. It looks like the UK hasn't taken us off the red list yet and tourism will remain in the toilet until they do.

The plug in my office broke. Of course it did. This shit always happens when you're at your busiest and most broke. Now have an extension cord running from the bedroom to my office.

Went to the Lastborn's induction at her school yesterday, I felt very emotional and off-kilter. But really appreciated it all. Wore a hat because I thought we would be in the quad where it's sunny, but we weren't. Looked like a tit, but so what? It gave me excellent material for this week's blog:

Embracing my weirdness

On Monday, I attended the Grade 11 induction service at the daughter's school. This is where the matrics hand over to the class below and there are solemn speeches about being a servant-leader. I do wish our political leaders had been there, they could've learnt a thing or two.

It was the first time we were back at the school since this shit-show began, and I felt like a dog that had just been let off its leash at the park, a dog that has never been to puppy obedience classes, bounding up to people trying to hug them, screaming, 'It's okay, I've had it and I'm a double-vaxxed kween!', while they valiantly tried to sidestep me like Lukhanyo Am did with the All Blacks in the Rugby Championship last weekend. The problem is that I have forgotten how to behave in social situations, I am literally like that woman who's been living with wolves for the last ten years and has emerged in need of a mani, pedi, a facial and some lessons in etiquette.

As soon as the Grade 10s started singing their beautiful song whose name I have forgotten because I have Covidy-menopausal brain, I started to blub. Then my nose started running underneath my mask. Naturally, I had no tissues but was rescued by a good Samaritan whom we shall call Ann because that is her name, and I was spared having to blow my nose on my one of the many discarded masks in my handbag. Yes, I am sexy like that.

I was grateful to the headmistress, who admitted that she also felt very emotional at this first event that parents could attend since the start of the pandemic. We started with a minute's silence for a family who had just lost their dad in a terrible accident but who insisted that the ceremony went ahead anyway (my heart!). Plus, my daughter's art was up in the hall – portraits of women and girls who have been killed in gender-based violence – which did not help matters. I felt the presence of the dead.

There was something about the occasion that just brought to the fore everything we have all endured over these last twenty months, all that has been lost, including loved ones and I felt the weight of it.

One of the deputy head girls gave a fantastic speech about the class of 2022 being a year of firsts. It was witty and lovely, but my heart just went out to all these children and what they have missed out on. As I keep saying to my kids, and I say this to all of you too: 'Give yourselves a break, you have just lived through a pandemic FFS!!'

As we were leaving, I got a pic of the daughter with the new head girl. They have been together at school since grade 0 and honestly, she is the loveliest person, and you could not find a better example of a servant-leader. I asked where her parents were, and she replied, 'They had to go, but it's fine,' opening her arms wide to include all of us, 'because I have all my parents here.'

I lay on the floor and wept some more.

Wednesday
DAY 149

What I have had a really great yearning for (besides a large glass of Optima) is the money to make sure the Lastborn can entertain like the rest of her friends. I want us to have a proper Christmas holiday. I want her to have a fantastic 18th and a beautiful matric dance. I want her to really enjoy her last year at school.

If the Husband gets this job, it will give us a chance to do all that.

I kind of feel fatalistic about it but keep chanting, 'I approach the future with curiosity', which is something I picked up in my morning meditation. Or perhaps on Instagram? Whatevs. I do feel curious about what the future will bring. I'm also excited about change, and new experiences.

We've been dreaming about the holidays that we'd like to take. One thing is sure: I feel unbelievable levels of gratitude now for things I took completely for granted ten, fifteen years ago. When you have struggled as much as we have and worked as hard as I have, you appreciate stuff so much more. As I wrote this, I realised I haven't written down a gratitude list for a while. So here goes:

I'm grateful for:

- This opportunity for the Husband
- That this has given us hope
- All the work I have
- That Christmas is coming
- My sobriety
- The thought that I might be able to provide a nice Christmas and holiday for my kids.

Jacaranda blossoms are starting to come out.

Friday
DAY 151

He got it!

HE GOT IT!!

A three-month contract for lots of lovely lolly. It's in Pretoria, which will be hectic – although at least he can take the Gautrain.

Of course, at the same time this happened, it seems Show 2 has come back from the dead like Lazarus. The new head writer (who is a fave) wants to start working on Monday. I feebly tried to tell him I was just too busy until the end of November.

His response: Fuck Show 1, I need you here.

Anyway, it will all work out as it should.

Beautiful stormy, rainy weather.

Sleep is an optional extra at the moment, I'm afraid.

Just got a script from Show 2 that has to be in on Monday at 9. Eeek! Let me work.

Wait. Did have the thought that with the Husband being out of the house from seven in the morning till about six in the evening, I will actually get a shitload done because I won't have anyone to walk with or gossip to.

Anyway, that's the theory!

Sunday
DAY 153

Can't help feeling the awesomey, Christmas feeling now that the jacarandas are coming out. Seven weeks until my contract with Show 1 ends. Of course, the work will not be finished then, it will spill over into the following week. But still . . . the end is in sight.

Aha moment: I am actually happiest working and spending time with my family, travelling, having experiences than just having parties and getting off my face all the time.

Wednesday
DAY 153

I went to my first in-person story meeting yesterday in 18 months. It was for Show 2 and I felt like peeps were not happy to see me, which made me start questioning why and made me get all anxious and full of people-pleasingness. There was also this weird anti-vaxxer sentiment that creeped me out.

We have had a week of loadshedding. Plus, the Parkhurst transformer thingie tripped last night. The power was out for seven continuous hours last night. The food I took out of the freezer was supposed to be cooked in the oven and ended up being cooked on the braai, so we only ate after eight. The Husband's first week at a job in Pretoria. Our lives are madness at the moment. Back to working on three shows, wondering when the hell we'll have time to edit our book, and I've agreed to do an author interview on 18th November.

Yes, I am insane. The problem with being a freelancer is that you do have to keep hustling to make sure you have work when your contract ends.

But let's be honest, I work this hard not just for the money but because I'm still trying to get daddy to notice me.

I remember being at my sister's house in Vic Falls, and my dad watching a local show on TV.

'Why aren't you in that?' he asked, accusingly.

Me: 'Well, I guess I'm just not good enough.'

I mean, what could I say? 'Sorry, Dad but I'm a failure?' He then went on to tell me that my hair, which I'd dyed blonde for my 30th birthday didn't suit me and that he didn't like it. It tickles me in a way that all my success happened once he'd died. Take that, sucker! I wasn't so useless after all.

I've tried so many things over the years and felt like such a failure when they didn't work out. It's only now that I've put all the puzzle pieces together and realised that nothing is ever wasted. That was my theme for this week's blog:

Nothing is ever wasted

When we're young, it can feel like we've wasted a whole lot of time and energy on dreams that never came to fruition. I was desperate to be a ballet dancer. I adored dancing, never mind that I didn't have the physique or the feet for it. I can remember doing a week of workshops at the National Ballet Centre in Harare and one of the guest teachers saying, 'Your top half is great, but the bottom—' She shook her head sadly. Reader,

I can only assume she was referring to my substantial ass. Funny now, not quite so amusing at age 14.

(Aside: why does ARSE sound so much ruder than ASS? One of life's little mysteries.)

I poured so much energy into my ballet. I was horrible at exams and would just scrape through, but I was great at performing. Then in my matric year, I was in the middle of doing a plié (same WhatsApp group as a squat but more graceful) and I remember thinking, 'this bores me'. It was kind of devastating because dancing had been my dream for so long, like, what was I if I wasn't a dancer?

But it was also a bit of an eye-opener because once I stepped back from it, I realised there was more to life than dancing, that in fact a large proportion of the world did not give a rat's ass (or even a rat's arse) about ballet. So I toddled off to varsity, feeling a bit anchorless, but then in the drama department I discovered contemporary dance and all my ballet skills suddenly didn't seem like such a waste at all. I ended up majoring in dance and using those same dance skills when I finally took a bash at making a career as an actor.

Sadly, the same thing happened with me with acting. We were doing the umpteenth performance of some show and once again I thought, 'this bores me'. Despite finding a great agent, I didn't really shoot the lights out as an actor. I would describe myself as mildly, rather than wildly, successful. I would like to blame my ass, but I'm not sure that was the only issue. I don't think my heart was in it, to be honest. Again, when the work fizzled out, I felt like a failure, like I had wasted all that time. I suspect at this point there might have been mutters of 'Time to get a real job' from my family, which I studiously ignored.

My acting career lead to me to starting my own educational kids' theatre company. I thought it would turn me into a Pieter Torien-style impresario. I didn't turn into any kind of impresario. When I didn't want to pay the lovely lady a bribe at Rand Water, our contract wasn't renewed and the company kind of fizzled out. Again, I felt like I'd wasted all that time.

But that writing of scripts led me to writing a musical for my master's thesis, which in turn led to my son's kindermusik teacher coming to watch, which led to me getting a shot at writing scripts for a local TV show.

I'd like to say, the rest is history, and we could have a nice montage here of me in the writers' room and pounding away on my laptop and being shat upon by the head writer for putting in too many exclamation marks and not enough action in my first script. Lord have mercy, that first script – it was truly horrible, but seeing my name up in the credits was pretty cool.

TV writing has not been an altogether smooth ride. This time it has nothing to do with my ass. But I can see now, with the benefit of hindsight, how one job has led me to the next in an unplanned way. I have used skills acquired from one job for the next.

I could see that quite clearly with my writing. How screenwriting has made me a better novelist, and vice versa, and how my acting and stand-up comedy skills have helped me during story meetings when I'm pitching a story or during book launches and interviews.

I think this is extremely pertinent now after we've just lived through this shitshow where we're all thinking, 'WT actual F is the point of trying to find meaning in things that are random. Like the pandemic?' It's been bloody hard, and it feels like the most incredible waste of two years. For me, it's too soon to answer that question and I know some people will say the only meaning of the pandemic is the one we assign to it, which is also fine. It is natural to want to see some great cosmic plan in everything.

Today, I am just grateful we are out of the third wave, that most of us in my household are vaccinated, that I have work, that we are healthy, that the jacaranda blooms are out and starting to look magnificent, that I will see some of my family members in December. I hope to get a break from work sometime before I turn 60, and NO, UNIVERSE, I AM NOT COMPLAINING ABOUT HAVING TOO MUCH WORK. Keep it coming. But beyond that, who knows? And that's the exciting bit.

I approach the future with curiosity.

Monday
DAY 161

Sister-in-law Sands's birthday today (Reader, this same person is also my beloved accountant and is the one person who manages to have just two G&Ts at events and that's it. An absolute model of moderation.) Just saw Amy for coffee. We were speaking about boundaries. So, so important and so difficult for those of us who have grown up in houses where there's been addiction to have these difficult convos. Because if we have the difficult conversations we might piss off our caregivers and be abandoned. I realise I often get the feeling with other writers that I'm being left behind. This is mostly ridiculous. I have work coming out of my ears, we've won a writing award this year, but it's my father's voice in my head constantly telling me I'm not good enough. I also blame social media for this, that we feel like everyone else is living these incredible lives.

Can't believe we survived a week of the Husband working in Pretoria despite having only the one car, loadshedding until Thursday, no water on Friday and no internet from Friday to Sunday.

Absolute madness.

The Husband took a sleeping pill and slept in the spare room last night. It meant I finally got some sleep, because he was snoring in another room. There's a lot to be said for separate rooms.

As things have eased off for us financially, I'm more aware of the suffering around me. People earning very little, or having no job and no hope.

Tuesday
DAY 162

We are going to be editing eight scripts for Show 2 a week. How the actual fuckitty-fuck that's going to work, I do not know. What I do know is that I might be invoicing lots and lots of moolah for November. That makes me incredibly happy. Whoever said money didn't buy happiness was smoking crack. Money gives you freedom and options. We're not talking billionaire-level money here, just comfortable middle-class contentment.

The poor Lastborn is losing her mind, she has so much work. You just want to make your kids feel better, but what you actually have to do is give them the tools to cope and guide them about making decisions.

Do often wonder if my issues with people don't say more about me than they do about them. What if I just accepted people for what they were? If I didn't expect them to be perfect? What if I just had fun with someone without requiring them to have every quality I need in a friend? I feel like I need to be more tolerant.

I want to live my life as if everyone is trying their best, not assume that peeps are out to get me.

Wednesday
DAY 163

Horrible gastritis yesterday.

Actually grew a pair and told management that I'm not feeling well this morning and went and slept at lunchtime for two hours. Still a bit headachy but at least stomach is feeling better.

Saw lovely friend Katherina this morning. Lord, but she has been through the mill. Married to a delicious man but they live in different countries. Her ex is not well so she has to pay for everything for the kids, and I mean everything. Works like an absolute dog and can only get by because she earns in dollars. It's crazy. But she is amazingly chipper about it all and has created a fantastic life for herself. An inspiration to me.

Wednesday
DAY 163

I told the Husband I was miffed that he could walk into a job and earn a big fat salary, that I have to work all hours god sends to try and match what he's earning. This is the difference between having an MA (me) and an MBA (him). And he is a man, which always helps. Hello, wage gap.

After I'd finished whining, I had the realisation that I try and kill myself to reach impossible deadlines, people-pleasing all the way, not trusting in my worth instead of saying, 'Well, actually no . . . getting XXX number of scripts out in the next month is fucking impossible. You may as well just take one of my kidneys right now.'

Okay, I'm not sure how giving them one of my kidneys would help get the script out, but you get my drift.

Obvs, I couldn't turn work down when the Husband wasn't earning anything, I just had to grit my teeth and get on with it. But if we do start coming out of this financial hole, that is my next aim. To not kill myself with work.

Note: in case the universe is listening, I am not moaning about him having work. No, no, no. I am extremely pleased about that. Just wish women and artists could be paid what they're worth.

Thursday
DAY 164

The good thing about having kids is that they provide excellent material, although one does have to get their sign-off now on everything you write about them and every picture you post on Facebook or the Gram. When they were little, it didn't occur to me that they might have strong feelings about this. We were very naïve about the socials back in the day. Now, we have been cancelled a few times by our own children and we know better. Managed to turn very amusing chat with the Firstborn into a blog, thanks god because I was scraping the bottom of the barrel as far as ideas go:

Conversations with my son

THE SON: I thought I was having a stroke last night.
ME: Oh no, why?
HIM: Firstly, I was so full, I had heart palpitations.
ME: Okay. Maybe that pizza was a bad idea.
HIM: It was. You know I made myself that big fried breakfast, then I ate some sushi with you guys, then I started eating the pizza and I was about four slices in, and I'd had enough.
ME: That's okay. Cold pizza is always good.
HIM: No, I finished it all, then I had a tub of Paul's ice cream.
*I am thinking how f*cking stupid this is, but I am far too old and wily to say that. This is not my first rodeo.*
ME: Oh dear . . . and that gave you heart palpitations?
HIM: (Some medical word about his blood) that my heart was battling to pump it around my body. Also, I had insomnia the whole night.
ME: Do you think perhaps it was a side-effect of your Covid vaccine?
HIM: No. It was definitely over-eating.
ME: I'm sorry to hear it. When we know better, we do better.
Yes, I said that with a straight face. My career as an actor was NOT WASTED.
HIM: And when I woke up, the internet was STILL out so I couldn't even watch YouTube or listen to a podcast. *Tragic expression* I had to read.
ME *without a trace of sarcasm*: How horrible for you. But I thought you were enjoying *Six Years With Al Qaeda.*
The son saw the cover of the book and went, 'Isn't that a St John's College old boy? We used to pray for him every day in Chapel. He better not have died. We did A LOT of praying.'

HIM: I am. Having no internet for two days is pretty much like Stephen McGown spending six years with Al Qaeda.

ME *without a trace of sarcasm*: Exactly the same. Like Jacob Zuma's fingers[5]. So, heart failure, insomnia, internet withdrawal. You still haven't explained about the stroke.

SON: Well, I woke up and smelt burnt popcorn.

ME: And that means you're having a stroke?

SON: No, that's burnt toast. But same WhatsApp group. I smelt burnt popcorn and the sourness of the salt and vinegar stuff Ruby was putting on it and then I smelt dad's cologne – I have a very strong sense of smell – and I was convinced I was (some other long medical word) and that I was either having a psychotic break or a stroke. But of course, I couldn't get up to research it because we had no internet.

ME: Imagine if you'd just had a textbook you could've picked up and read?

No, dear Reader, I did not say that, but I did think it. I also did wonder why this boy was doing a medical research degree and not a drama degree.

Our internet was down from midday Friday to Sunday morning, and I have to admit that we were a bit lost without it. There was no TikTok, no YouTube, no Netflix, no Apple TV, because, evil parents that we are, we were not going to cough up to buy data for any of those. Not when we have a house filled with books that could be read.

I was gazing at our one bookshelf on Sunday morning, thinking how thrilled I would've been if we'd had this many books in our house growing up. There were books we just couldn't buy in Zimbabwe when I was young. I can remember walking into a shop when we were on holiday in South Africa and nearly fainting from joy because I could buy the latest Enid

5 The famous meme where Jacob Zuma is laughing and pressing his index fingers together.

> Blyton. I assumed my kids would share my obsession with reading. I was wrong.
>
> The son won a prize at prep school for reading the most books for the term. He did, however, approach it like the scientist that he is. He worked out how many pages he could read in a week, chose the shortest possible books and, hey presto, he won the big fat chocolate for Most Books Read and possibly some kind of badge. He was a complete badge whore and would join every possible band in the music department so he could get a new, shiny badge. After the reading prize, I of course, thought he would be an avid reader for life. Nope. Didn't happen. This used to upset me, in the sense of *I read to you while you were in the womb, I read you stories every night, we still love the story of* Walter the Farting Dog *and yet you do not like reading. Where did I go wrong*?!
>
> I did not go wrong. Well, not about that. I went wrong in many other respects, but the thing is, our children are not us. They are themselves, with their own likes and dislikes and their own journeys to take. The son has now decided, due to his love of podcasts (author Boykey Sidley introduced him to, thanks Boyks!), that non-fiction audio books are for him because he reckons he loves finding out about other people's lives.

Cool, cloudy day today. Been a bit of a chilly spring although supposed to have a hot weekend. Let's see.

Friday
DAY 165

First meeting with our editor about the group novel. Eeeeek! Some interesting insights into the character that I wrote – whose name I could not remember. God! This is a thing BTW. After your first novel, much like your kids and your cats, you do not remember the names of your beloved characters. Or the plot. Or indeed the title.

Weird thing happened last night. Schim's book launch didn't take place because there was a bomb scare at Rosebank. Second one this week. The Lastborn heard at school that there would be shit at various malls in the run-up to the elections. The Husband wondered if she's hanging out with a group of mafiosos that she has this info. Ho hum.

Horrible for Schim and very disappointing for the rest of us who were looking forward to a night out. In South Africa, we're all busy getting vaxxed and looking forward to summer so it's ominous to see infection numbers climbing in the UK and an outbreak in China.

Will this bloody thing ever calm down?

Am exceedingly tired of Covid.

And if anyone tells me that I might be tired of Covid, but Covid is not tired of me, I will punch them.

In the face.

Saturday
DAY 166

Just got an invite to have bubbles under the star jasmine at the house of lovely bookish mate Tamara (LePine-Williams). Tamara and I met when she had a book show on Classic FM. We had some hilarious moments together, which included her asking me (on live radio) who some of the characters in my second book were based on (our kids went to the same schools, and we know a lot of the same people), while I kept shaking my head and making 'I am going to get you' gestures. We also had a superb dinner with author Lesley Pearse at the Franschhoek Lit Fest, organised by my then work Husband, Ryno Posthumus. I had a raging hangover the next day and had to take two Disprin before my panel, which included international author Joanne Harris and one of my favourite local authors, Jo Macgregor. Interviewer Victor Dlamini wickedly started reading out my tweets while I clutched my head and groaned. I can't pretend that these moments weren't the most fun, but I also realise that those days are over for me.

I turned down the invite for bubbles because the Lastborn has a water polo tournament and she also needs to get her art stuff in. We need to be here for her and cook her a nutritious dinner. When I was drinking, I would've happily organised take-aways and buggered off and got roaringly drunk. Now, I realise how frequently I dropped the ball as a parent.

For instance, instead of joining the Firstborn on his tour of his high school, thinking that he only had one school on his list anyway, we happily dropped him off and went to Red Wine Friday at our mates' house. Turns out it wasn't the best fit for him school-wise. Would we have realised that from a tour? Probably not. But I still think of that day. I resolve to do better as a parent.

As we drove through the St Stithians gates this morning, I turned to the Husband and said, 'We have one more year of this and then we're done, we probably won't come to these schools again.'

It was such a wow moment. You cannot get this time back with your kids. It's over. The Lastborn is so independent that I've often just left her to her own devices, which is wrong. Even though she was the kid who insisted on lighting her own birthday candles at playschool (much to the teacher's horror), would not let us walk her into school for her first day at 'big' school and whose personal motto has always been 'I can do it', she still needs her parents just as much as any other kid does.

Aside: I still don't like lighting matches. Distant cousins from Durban were playing in a house they had made out of a cardboard box and set it alight and got badly burnt. My mother then took a match, blew it out and pressed the embers to my hand to show me how fire could hurt me. I think I was four.

This was not unusual back in the day. I remember someone advising me to prick my son with a pin if he went near a plug point.

Oh-kay.

Sunday
DAY 167

Halfway through the Lastborn's swimming tournament – at which her team got clobbered – we were told that we were allowed to attend. I wrote about how wonderful it was in this week's blog, after 18 months of not being allowed to watch our kids playing sport:

ME *as I went in for the hug*: are we allowed to do this?

OTHER PARENT: We are using protection, it's fine (we were both wearing masks).

Not knowing who people are under their masks is something I still battle with. I don't recognise anyone and the Husband can't hear a word anyone is saying. We make an attractive pair of old dodderers. I sat for a full ten minutes staring blankly at a woman who seemed vaguely familiar and I realise why she was so familiar after another mate introduced us. Turned out to be the daughter's teacher from her old prep school whom I know very well.

There was a lot of reminiscing at the match. We remembered how we moaned at the endless games we had to watch; now we were ecstatic to get up at the crack of dawn and sit by the pool watching our team lose. Yes, you heard me right: we knew we weren't going to do brilliantly because, tragically, our wonderful young goalie broke her thumb, and so various other members of the team – including the daughter – with no goalie experience had to stand in for her.

They did this with good cheer, and I said to the one player, who was very sad about chalking up another loss, winning is easy. It's easy to be gracious and kind to your opponent when you're winning, but losing well shows true character. Not being bad losers, still having fun, not giving up even though the odds are against you – that's a true test of character. And let me tell you, they passed with distinction. As Brené Brown points out in her fabulous documentary *The Call To Courage* on Netflix, sometimes just finishing the race is winning.

The benefits of Covid are few and far between, but I feel that this is one of them. The participation in the sports' tournament, parents being allowed to watch, felt more important than who actually won.

Monday
DAY 168

Well, the onslaught has begun. I opened my computer this morning to find out that I have a script to hand in for Show 2 on Wednesday after which I will have eight scripts to edit. The best part, though, is that an old nemesis, whom I shall call Iago, is writing one of the scripts I'm going to edit. I suspect Iago is the reason I missed out on one job and got fired from another many moons ago.

But this is ancient history now.

I'm interested as to why this guy keeps turning up in my life and what lesson I am supposed to be learning here. Also, what am I supposed to do?

- ✔ Tell them I won't work with him?
- ✔ Ask for him to be moved to the other editor?
- ✔ Ignore it. Everyone deserves a second chance?

It would give me a lovely excuse to turn down this work that I'm ambivalent about, but it's not in my nature to do that and let people down. Also, I'm wondering if he does deserve a second chance at this point. I honestly don't know. Plus, I'm just too exhausted to cope with any drama and really, am I in a financial position to get fired from this job?

Not really.

Tuesday
DAY 169

Sister's 30th wedding anniversary today. Her wedding was in Harare and it was a humdinger. I was her bridesmaid in shocking-pink satin. It was the most beautiful spring day, hot, with thunder rumbling in the distance but no rain. Got so incredibly drunk at that wedding that I kept trying not to retch during the opening of the presents the next day.

Chilly, rainy weather. We're having a bit of a cold spring, but we need rain and TBH when you're up to your eyeballs in work, it's easier when it's cold.

Got awful notes about the eps on Show 1 this morning, but we carry on.

Thursday
DAY 171

Just got a script for Show 3 this morning. Due at COB tomorrow. Hysterical panic!

Have 500-odd kids coming past my house for Halloween on Saturday. No, I don't understand why I thought that would be a good idea on top of all my work. Gave the Lastborn a lecture about triage – addressing the most important thing first – now I have to live by those words. Just take each day as it comes and try get through it.

Have already got through shitload of work:

- ✔ Wrote half script for Show 3
- ✔ Finished blog
- ✔ Went for a walk, got coffee
- ✔ Edited four scripts for Show 1
- ✔ Two phone calls to sort out script issues on Show 1
- ✔ Edited one script for Show 2.

Still have a good four hours of work left in which I need to edit three more scripts for Show 2, identify scenes in Show 1 episodes for experts, make notes on the last scenes pulled for experts, and write three more scenes for episode for Show 3 (A script, dear Reader, is made up of 12 to 14 scenes).

Never. Fucking. Ends. Yoh!

Things I am grateful for today:

- ❤ The generator
- ❤ My son who can start the generator
- ❤ Jacaranda blossoms.

NOVEMBER

Monday
DAY 175

I am sipping a glass of fake champers after voting. It always feels like a momentous occasion to vote, something I never take for granted in South Africa, where this right was denied the majority for so long. We organised a fabulous Halloween stop for the neighbourhood's kids on Saturday. We put up all our decorations outside: an enormous furry spider in a web, a hanging decoration we refer to as Evil Angel and which cackles, another I call Groaning Ghoul, and a head on a stick we've named Dead Baby, plus loads of fake spiders' web with little spiders in it. Have I mentioned that I'm excessively arachnophobic?

We also got all dressed up for the occasion. I'm not quite sure the look I was going for: ancient bride? Dracula's mom? Anyway, lots of fake blood and white paint was required along with an outfit so synthetic that I was steering clear of any open flames and getting electric shocks every time I touched anything metal. The Husband set up a table outside, we had music pumping and had a frame with props where kids and their parents could take a hellfies (hell + selfie = hellfie. Geddit??) I spent a small fortune on sweets from the plastic shop but I have no regrets. I loved the joy on the kids' faces. They were all so well-behaved, I had to encourage them to take handfuls of sweets. I also ate about twenty fizzers. I shit you not.

We offered wine to a few friends who stopped by with their kids. I drank a bottle of fake champers, and I was dancing and thoroughly enjoying myself.

The very best part? It was over by 7.30.

I am going to miss curfew when it's finally abolished.

Work is INSANE at the moment but, as ever, I am grateful for it. Iago's script was beyond horrendous. So not only do I get to work with this prince, but I also get to rewrite his scripts AND give him notes to show him how to improve. God, I'd better be getting a few hundred years off from my time in purgatory for all this turn-the-other-cheek shite.

I managed to get through the first round of editing on my book. Feels great although it means I haven't had a day off from work this week. My shoulder seized yesterday so I went to the new Thai place in the village for a massage. It was worse than the chiropractor. This tiny woman, who did not speak one word of English, climbed on my back and literally fucked me up. I thought I was going to have to puke in the wastepaper bin from the pain but managed not to. Just. Hopefully it did the trick. I read in Amanda Kuda's emails about the necessity of finding other ways of coping with stress apart from reaching for the wine. Going for walks and killer massages are definitely up there for me.

I am about a week away from hitting six months of being sober curious. Huge milestone. I'll treat myself to something to celebrate. Maybe a bottle of perfume. We'll see.

Tuesday
DAY 176
All Souls' Day and the Day of the Dead

This is a day when, as Catholics, we remember our dead. Back in the day, when I used to go to church, we would even write the names of our deceased loved ones on little pieces of paper, which were then taken up to the altar. Thinking about Mom today. I am very pleased my life is not like hers. I am exceptionally grateful that I have an education and that I earn my own money.

It's something I keep drumming into the Lastborn. *Never be dependent on your partner. Always earn your own money.* Dad controlled Mom through money, dishing out a minute allowance as if she were a child. I never wanted to be in that position.

Lastborn's art exam didn't go well. Apparently, drawing is not for her. She has been an artist for as long as I can remember and has been approached by people online who've commissioned her to do digital art for them. I wish I could tell her how all this exam stuff doesn't matter, that she is actually talented beyond measure, and that she will discover that once she leaves academia. So hard to be young.

The head honcho at the Husband's company told him airily that he might not be needed after December. His contract is supposed to go on until the end of February, so we're both trying not to freak out. Hopefully, it's not true. But if it does happen, holding thumbs that Go See Do starts picking up. How lucky we are to have GSD as an option.

Ha! I say that as if the company is earning money. It is not. I just try to be optimistic. Also, if I think too much about it, I want to have a panic attack, so I push it out of my mind. There's also not much else I can do, I can't work any more hours than I'm currently working.

Gorgeous weather. May go for a quick swim now.

Later: ended up working and never did have that swim. *Quelle surprise.*

Thursday
DAY 178

Went to A Streetbar Named Desire last night for Desdemona's birthday. Had a nice chat with Miranda. She was amazed that I'm six months off the grog. She said something interesting to me: that she never would've pegged me as someone who had a problem with alcohol. But that's just it. We live in a society that is positively marinaded in vino, so it's hard to tell who has a problem and who doesn't.

I drank a virgin mojito and some other unspeakable virgin cocktail that cost a ridiculous amount of money and tasted like sugar water. The Husband had three beers and has a hangover today.

I might've felt the teensiest bit smug this morning as he clutched his aching head. I'm tired but no hangover.

Friday
DAY 179

It's been confirmed. The Husband's contract that was supposed to go until the end of Feb is now finishing at the end of December. He looked like he'd been kicked in the stomach when he told me.

Felt verrrrrrrry pissed off, but then gave myself a little pep talk. Our book editor is donating her kidney to her child next Friday. What are my problems in comparison to that? Nothing.

The Husband has an income for two more months. He needs to get other projects off the ground in the meantime. Life is good.

Later: hotshot lawyer friend has told the Husband that the company doesn't have a leg to stand on, so let's see. He may have to accept a compromise and be paid until the end of Jan. The unpleasantness of having to fight with people. It's exhausting.

Saturday
DAY 180

Went to Red Wine Friday at Miranda's last night. Turned out to be rather nice. I am starting to learn what it's like to socialise without a toot and it's fine. What helped was having an interesting and eclectic group of people to talk to. I took my dealc'd champers along and sipped on that. The only problem is, one tends to drink the whole bottle in a couple of hours and then you feel like Walter-the-Farting-Dog, filled with hot air and about to rise to the ceiling. (It really is an excellent book, Reader. I still read it aloud to my adult kids and we all piss ourselves laughing.)

Went to Rosebank to try and find some perfume to buy myself to celebrate sixth months of temperance, but soon got overwhelmed and couldn't choose. Also smelt like a cheap hooker by the end of it.

Ended up chatting to the saleslady at Woolies about her experience of Covid. As she said, 'Thank God we both survived it.'

Since the pandemic, things suddenly have very little value. What I crave is experiences.

Apparently, numbers are starting to go up again. Hello, fourth wave.
Going to be a stinker of a day today. Will this finally be the day I get out there by the pool?

Monday
DAY 182

The Husband is going to have a showdown with head honcho from the UK today. I feel for him. It's all so unpleasant. I run from conflict.

What this comes back to, though, is that we don't have fuck-you money and that is an issue. Everybody needs fuck-you money. This concept was first introduced to us by the editor of *TIME Atlantic,* Chris Redmond (the Husband worked for *TIME* for many years). Clearly, I was pissed and not paying attention when he said it because we did not listen to him. Basically, one should never be in so much debt that you can't walk away from a shitty work situation. I think I wrote that in the Lastborn's 21st birthday card. If I can teach our kids anything, it's to not get into the stupid amount of debt we've got into. We have to finish launching our kids into the world and then hopefully we can worry about our finances.

Thursday
DAY 185

Yesterday I hit the precise sixth month mark for my sober curious journey. I went to Schim's book launch of *Never Tell A Lie,* where I would usually have been tossing the champers down my throat, but I held back. Instead, two Diet Cokes (caffeine so late not a good idea, but still). In spite of Schim moaning that no one was going to come, it was packed. Sue Nyathi was the discussant, and she was wonderful. All the books were sold out, plus the *Chasing Marian* crew got a little mention. Qarnita is based in Cape Town, so the Husband made a cardboard cut-out of her so we could include her in the photographs, which added to the fun. Author Fiona Snyckers was there and was so lovely about both my blog and the psychological thriller that I'm working on (okay, I haven't worked on it for a verrrrrrrry long time) that I felt quite full of myself.

The most important take-away, however, was that you can have fun without booze.

I didn't sleep well (probs the caffeine in the Coke), but at least that wasn't compounded by having a hangover. In days gone by, I would've woken up with a pounding head, probably have had to suck down a few Disprins before I could function. Not this time.

My system is more sensitive with sobriety. The alcohol was masking certain physical things and numbing others, and this was also true emotionally. I now often feel exposed and raw. I have to give myself little talking-tos so that I don't overreact to things and think people are looking at me funny when in reality they're really not looking at me at all.

The Husband has had a hellish week but eventually told the Head Honcho on Tuesday evening that he has a contract and will be staying until the end of February, finish and klaar! The way this dickhead has treated the Husband is a good lesson on how not to use employees like pieces on a chessboard. Looks like I will be working my ass off until December 16th. I'll have two weeks off then and who knows when Show 1 will start in the new year. Everything is so uncertain.

I am fed up with working so hard all the time. We've been thrown so many curveballs over the last 12 years that I can't relax at all. I know this is the essence of mindfulness – to be okay with whatever comes your way – but I am tired.

PS: The Firstborn was so helpful yesterday and picked up champers and some very beautiful flowers for Schim, and did some shopping for me. I was quite impressed.

Sunday
188 DAYS

Read another great quitlit book called *Glorious Rock Bottom* by Bryony Gordon. Found it both funny and moving and could relate to some of the stuff she was saying. Oddly, she did not think of the awkward situations she found herself in as sexual assault. They were. Made me think about myself and the situations I've put myself in.

Exhibit A

I am 14 and have never French-kissed anyone. I'm at a party at one of my siblings' digs. I am dressed in a pink satin body suit, big white shirt, pink legwarmers and white stilettos. (It was so very 80s.) I look way older and have had something to drink. I end up slow dancing with a 19-year-old and French-kissing him. He is absolutely gorgeous and keeps asking me to go outside. Luckily, at this point I realise that going outside with him would be a bad idea. I decline. After the party, he phones often to ask me out. I am always unavailable.

Note: no one blinks an eye at the fact that he is 19 and I am 14.

Exhibit B

I am in my first year at university and at a house party. I'm off my trolley drunk. The boyfriend of one of the older students is flirting with me, which I am definitely enjoying, especially when he tells me that he saw me in the dance programme and how fabulous I was. What I enjoy less is when he gets me alone in one of the bedrooms, pushes me back on the bed and starts giving me oral sex. One of the other students walks in and interrupts us. Thank God. Who knows what would've happened? The next day I am deeply ashamed and blame myself for getting into that situation. I don't even question what an attached man three years my senior was doing trying to get lucky with a 17-year-old virgin.

Exhibit C

Still a virgin, just. It's the end of first year and I'm working as a waitress at a pizza place. We are waitresses but also dancers. The owner has put a stage upstairs and wants to have shows there. On the carpet upstairs is where I will lose my virginity – to the owner, a 34-year-old, who's been married three times and whose current wife is 23. I am, once again, off-my-face drunk. The wife of this lovely specimen, after she finds out about this affair, mentions how she could tell I was trouble from the moment she met me. I agree that I am trouble. It does not occur to me that perhaps the 34-year-old, who is (I regret to say) shagging just about all the waitresses in the establishment, is the troublesome one.

This, unfortunately, is a situation that would repeat itself over and over again.

Older, attached, emotionally abusive men?

Yes, please, I'll have two of those!

And alcohol was always involved.

Many, many years later, when the Firstborn turned 18 and I saw just how very young 18 is, and how lacking in sense 18-year-olds are (that prefrontal cortex is only fully developed at 25), I reflected on the experience with the 34-year-old Lothario. What made me sad is that my mother overheard a conversation I was having with him and worked out that we were involved. But instead of sending my father around there with a shotgun, she called me every name under the sun and would not talk to me because I was such a harlot. This is what makes me very grateful for the Husband. If that was either of our kids, there would not be anywhere for a man like that to hide. He would be found and dealt with. And no, the Husband would not be using his words, he would be using his fists. Well, perhaps a few choice words along with his fists.

Monday
DAY 189

Feeling a bit sad today. Not sure why. Got up, went for a walk, did some weights and meditated. Maybe it's just the neverendingness of my workload?

Or it could be that my weight was 71.1 this morning. No, no and no.

I need to get back to intermittent fasting, and only eating fruit and berries, a little yoghurt until supper.

Maybe just give up eating altogether?

Gorgeous weather this week. Had a very delish swim after supper last night.

Used hair removal cream on beard/tache. Honestly, the beard and the wiry, black hairs on my chin are getting completely out of control. I look like I'm transitioning. To what, I'm not entirely sure. A werewolf perhaps?

FOUR. MORE. WEEKS.

Friday
193 DAYS

Did my first in-person interview since Auntie Rona at Exclusive's Rosebank last night with debut author Michelle Edwards. Because of Covid, there was no vino and no snacks, just a few cooldrinks, which felt like a bit of a downer for the poor author and audience. Still, *Go Away Birds* is a stunning book and I think it went well. One thing hasn't changed since giving up the grog: I still experience a terrible downer after these events. I suspect it has something to do with the adrenaline leaving my body. It's not very pleasant. I always thought it was the booze, alas but apparently it wasn't that. Also, battled to sleep last night, it takes me a while to unwind after these events.

Got the edits back for *Chasing Marian* a week early. Apparently, I have met this editor before – at the very first in-conversation I ever did with author Paige Nick. It was the *Dutch Courage* launch at Beefcakes, where I was dressed in my underwear and ended the evening licking shooters off some poor chap's stomach.

On brand, really.

I should be revelling in all this bookish stuff, but I'm too exhausted to think of it as anything more than another thing to add to my to-do list.

Was asked by Penguin to write a nice thing about Marian Keyes for their local mag. Dying to spill the beans about our book, but we haven't done a title reveal yet or explained what it's about so will still have to keep my trap shut.

Am going to have to work with a new head writer on one of our shows. The script editor and the head writer have to work very closely together so I always worry when there's a new one 'cause if they're not nice, life can become very unpleasant. Time will tell.

Read an interesting blog about a poverty mindset and never being able to stop working because you're scared of being poor. Hmmm. *Change the story you tell yourself and you can change your life.* Where did I read that? Or did I get it off TikTok? Possibly.

Covid cases in Gauteng are starting to rise. Fourth wave here we come. Woo-hoo!

Sunday
DAY 195

Am in a very this-too-shall-pass frame of mind. Did most of my edits on the book and have worked out that Sunday midday means 3.5 weeks to go until I'm done. I can get through it. I just need to keep putting one foot in front of the other and taking care of myself.

I like to have little fantasies imagining that one of my books is this smash hit that makes a huge amount of loot, and I actually get to take some time off. Except then I read a thing by bestselling author Jojo Moyes (remember *Me Before You*?) saying that she hasn't had more than a week off in three years, so I think it's probably more like that. I think once you're a freelancer, even when you're making millions, you're too terrified of turning work down in case you never work again. That's definitely true for me.

Cool, cloudy weather for the next few days. Gorgeous thunderstorm yesterday.

THREE. AND A HALF. WEEKS. That is all.

And they will whizz by.

Got the Save The Date for the nephew's wedding. It's going to be next August in Scotland; I cannot wait to see my extended family again. Babies have been born during Covid that I have yet to meet. I will see beloved nieces, Kiks and Nade. Haven't seen them in forever. (They're both teachers, Reader, and one is in London and the other in Australia.) They are so kick-ass and gorgeous and fun. I miss them both terribly. How we are going to pay for the trip is, however, a mystery.

Wednesday
DAY 198

Yesterday we got an email from Show 2 saying that we no longer have to produce all these hundreds of scripts for them by the end of the year. It does mean things calm down a little and I'll be able to give Show 1 the attention it deserves. I felt a bit down thinking about the money I would lose out on, but I'm also so exhausted that mostly I felt relief. Tonight, I'll hand in the last of the edits on the novel. It's a good feeling to be able to start winding down. Also, Iago's scripts have really improved, so there's that. Why do I even care? I know, I know, but it's the teacher in me. I can't help myself.

The Firstborn's exam was a nightmare, he tells me. He is prone to catastrophising, so I really, really hope he's exaggerating, and he passes and gets his degree because he keeps insisting that if he fails, he's not redoing the year. Ho-hum. Had to restrain myself from telling him a few hard truths about the unemployment rate in the country.

The Lastborn's last exam tomorrow but then she has a swimathon, the matric dance and house plays to get through before she finishes.

She is, alas, a workaholic like her dear mama.

I really do need to be a better role model.

Friday
200 DAYS

The 33rd anniversary of when the Husband and I moved in together at the end of my last year of my first degree. We both came from very strict Catholic families so there was general horror at the thought of us Living In Sin. I was shopping with my mother in Maritzburg when she turned to me and said, 'Are you . . . shacked up with him?' in a sort of Lady Bracknell tone of voice that made it sound like I had just produced a dead rat from my handbag. We were also not received for lunch at a very religious aunt's house because we were so tainted.

Pens down dinner with the fam last night at Turn 'n Tender. The Lastborn had just finished her exams. Apparently, she got a leetle creative with that last history paper. The Firstborn has (hopefully!) finished his degree. His last paper was also a bit of a train smash. We've handed in the last edits on the novel. It now goes off to Marian to see if she approves. Eeeeek!

Ordered a glass of wine at dinner – the first glass I've had since August. Drank half of it. Heart started to race, and I felt a headache coming on so gave the rest to the Husband and gulped down water and eventually the sensations receded.

God. I think I may literally be allergic to alcohol. Or at least cheap booze. It definitely wasn't as enjoyable as the glass at Marble. Ate so much that I battled to sleep. Kept going through a plot point in one of the scripts at three in the morning.

The major realisation was that I don't have to finish a glass of wine. I can order a glass of wine for 60 bucks or 90 bucks, or even 200 bucks, and have a few sips and not finish it. It is really up to me. Seems fairly obvious to anyone else but it was mind-blowing for me. We were brought up to finish every scrap on our plates and were served that leftover cabbage for breakfast if we didn't finish it the night before. Not that anyone in my house ever didn't finish the booze. That was definitely not an issue in my household, but there was that mindset that you do not waste, and for me that extended to not wasting wine.

Huge relief because I no longer need to help out on editing for Show 2. No more of Iago's terrible scripts to rewrite. No, no, let me be fair, even his scripts have improved. And I've got at least a century or two off my time in purgatory. Woo-hoo. So, current workload:

- ✔ Write two scripts a week
- ✔ First edit on eight scripts for Show 1
- ✔ Final edit on ten scripts for Show 1
- ✔ Write blog for Go See Do.

We are now most probably going into the fourth wave of Covid in Gauteng, and they have found a new variant. Looks like our family Christmas party won't happen as we've been put on the red list for the UK. So the fam won't come through here on their way to Zambia. Just feel a kind of weary resignation.

Lastborn's school are holding their matric dance (which should've happened in February) tomorrow night. Really hope it still happens for the girls' sake, but I suspect the interhouse plays next week might be cancelled. The Lastborn has worked so hard on the script, it would be a terrible blow. These kids have had to endure so much in the last two years, not just missing out on their schooling and the various rites of passage, but the ever-present fear of Covid and themselves or someone close to them getting sick and possibly dying.

Really, really hope the Lastborn has a more normal year next year. This is so hard on the kids.

ACT III

... or even two or three glasses

(December 2021 to February 2022)

DECEMBER

Wednesday
DAY 205

Matric dance happened after all, for which I am most thankful. What I am less thankful for is that she might have Covid. She said the dance floor felt like a seething Covid-y mass. All I can say is thanks god she has had one vaccine. Unfortunately, we all went to our local, Blind Tiger, last night with Maudie so that's not brilliant. I still feel filled with gorgeous immunity, so I think I'll be okay, but she's has never had Covid, in spite of all of her flitting around the world.

She is on her way back from Mauritius, where their company's headquarters is based, to her home in Victoria Falls. The way she describes Mauritius makes me want to go live there, especially considering the second bastardy rainy summer we're having. I think of the fullness of the Vaal Dam and try feel grateful, but I definitely need some sun.

(I've never been to Mauritius, Reader. I have only been to the Seychelles. I say only. Courtesy of my sister and my brother-in-law, the entire family went to a private island called North Island when the kids were small. I wasn't kidding when I said we've enjoyed some fairly stupendous holidays courtesy of my family.)

Thursday
DAY 206

Well, we are now in the fourth wave with the new Omicron variant (which I keep calling omnibus) and the Lastborn has Covid. I was very concerned about her on the first day because she really was (wo)man down, but she seemed a lot more chipper today. I'm putting that down to the vaccine. I started feeling fluey so went for a test, and so the Husband decided he had to go too. He seems desperate to get it as he keeps hugging the Lastborn even though I screech at him to stay away from her.

Have to admit that I did feel irritated that I might have it after being ill with Covid and being double-jabbed.

Had a publicity meeting about *Chasing Marian* yesterday, which was fun and just made it all feel so real. This is actually happening!

Am starting to lose my sense of humour with Show 1 as the one expert keeps contradicting what the other expert is saying, and it doesn't help when no one gets back to you on time, and you have eleventy-twelve billion scripts to issue. Arghhhhhhhh!

Also, wouldn't be at all surprised if one of the cast members tests positive for Covid and the production gets shut down. Show 3's already been shut down 'cause of Covid.

It is our wedding anniversary in two days' time. For the first time in – *adds on fingers* – 28 years I have not bought the Husband a present. I just have not had time. I'm drowning in work.

Friday
DAY 207

Still don't have test results but at least I am up and working, and I have 12 days of this shittiness to get through before I can take a break. So much for not having to do scripts for Show 2 – I am still editing but hopefully this is the last week of doing them. So workload in the 12 days until I go away consists of:

- ✔ Doing final edit on eight scripts for Show 2
- ✔ Doing final edit on ten scripts for Show 1
- ✔ Doing first edit on five scripts for Show 1.

And writing God-knows-how-many scripts. I have five earlier scripts from Show 1 that I need to tweak too. And they would really like me in the story room for Show 1. Do you fucking want these scripts delivered on time, or do you want me in the story room? Choose, motherfuckers!

No, I did not say that. But I did think it and may have shouted it into the ether.

Then I started stressing that if I could not be in two places at once, which I clearly should be able to be according to them, they'll be cross with me and won't like me. I went into this whole panic spiral even though I was feeling beyond irritated and as if my boundaries were being trampled by a whole herd of elephants.

I tried to sit with my discomfort. I always get too involved, throw myself heart and soul into whatever work I do. I've started weaning myself off that. This is a contract. Yes, it's for a show I adore. But if I died tomorrow, they would push my still-warm corpse out of the way so they could appoint the next editor.

That's the nature of the beast.

Also: in a week, a month, a year, none of this will matter.

Something like 11 500 infections last night. Majority in Gauteng. But only 44 deaths so we hope that there is some immunity from vaccines and previous infections.

The Husband had an intriguing suggestion from his mentor on the Enpact programme (the German programme we signed up for in August, the one that gave us the euros). It's about them going into business together. I'm so jaded my first response was: where's the money coming from? Second response: is this guy a scam artist?

Sunday
DAY 209

I am negative! Praise be. Vaccines do work.

The Lastborn is so much better. Huge relief. We're hovering around the 16k mark for infections but only twenty-odd deaths. These numbers seem to go up and down daily. It will obviously still rise but it's a sign that natural immunity and the vaccines are kicking in.

28th wedding anniversary yesterday: pissed with rain last night just like it did on our wedding day. The Husband bought me flowers and a soppy Helen Steiner Rice card, which cracked me up, and I bought him . . . nothing. Actually, not true. I bought him R400 worth of underpants from Woolies.

I always felt like our wedding was a bit of a disaster. It was held at the smallholding we were living on then just outside of Richmond in KZN and some people couldn't even get up the farm road in the mud. The Husband and I had a massive fight the night before, then I was half an hour late for the service because our cars got stuck in the mud going down the farm road and he thought I might not turn up. Which pleased me. I also got pissed and had a hangover the next day. Ugh.

Part of my anxiety was worrying about my mother getting drunk and being embarrassing. Something to remember when my own kids get married. TRY NOT TO BE EMBARRASSING. When she was drunk, my mother could be insanely embarrassing.

Exhibit A

We – my brother, my sister and I – go to a Sunday evening church service in Pietermaritzburg with my mother. She has been drinking all day and is irritated with us for some reason. Perhaps because we are late for Mass? We are late and she wants to sit in the front of the church (naturally), and we are happy hovering at the back. She finds a seat away from us, which turns out to be a blessing as she insists on clapping loudly when the priest says things she agrees with and even shouting the odd 'Yes!'

Exhibit B

Eugene Terreblanche is addressing his AWB supporters at the Town Hall in Maritzburg. We go to protest. My mother is drunk and completely stroppy. When he walks past her, she spits at him and swears at him in Afrikaans. Although this is kind of hilarious, she is extremely lucky she doesn't get taken out by one of his henchmen.

So thrilled that the Lastborn got five distinctions at the end of the year. This is a kid who never used to get As, but since she started taking subjects she loves – *voilà*!

Ten days to go until I can take a break. Very much looking forward to it. Had a day off yesterday after working for 21 days straight and it was heaven.

Monday
DAY 210

I got a psychologist to look through some of the shrink-y bits in *Chasing Marian* a coupla weeks ago. The hilarious thing was that he analysed the character and came up with wonderful insights. The not-so-hilarious part was that the character was created by me and so I had to examine those insights in relation to myself. The character is a young man who is very close to his mother but despises his alcoholic father. Shrink Richard pointed out that in fact the character was a lot angrier with his mother and was in fact projecting all that anger onto his father.

It was such an aha moment for me. I have never allowed myself to feel angry with my mother because I always felt so sorry for her being in such a shitty relationship. But why didn't she get a job? Why didn't she quit the grog? Why did she allow our father to treat us all like shit and move the family around so much?

There are no answers to these questions. My mother and father are long dead. It is once again interesting to me how alcohol anaesthetises a person and allows them to remain in a shitty situation instead of getting the hell out of it.

Perhaps just by having a job and her own money, her life would've been so much better.

I keep drumming into the Lastborn that she must always, always earn her own money, but I think I've been preaching to the wrong child.

Firstborn: All I want is a rich man.

Husband: Don't we all?

Ho-hum.

Tuesday
DAY 211

The Firstborn passed his degree! The Husband immediately suggested that he take him out for a drink. I vetoed that, ostensibly because the Lastborn is still in quarantine but mainly because we need to find other ways to celebrate instead of tossing booze down our throats. Maybe cake? But is that just feeding our sugar addiction? A meditation session?

Hahaha.

Was feeling thoroughly irritated with everyone on Show 1 because of them changing their minds and making us do rewrites when we are so stretched. Managed to be very sweet in the meeting yesterday, which I think helped calm everything down. Am going to show my face (actually my voice) at the Zoom story meeting this morning, stay for a couple of hours and then bugger off and do some work.

Tomorrow, we have a partial cover reveal for *Chasing Marian* and a sort of publicity thing on social media, which should be fun. The novel is the most fun thing to work on at the moment.

Nine days until I go on my break. Not that I'm counting, just saying.

Praying that Oom Cyril doesn't ban interprovincial travel. I need some Vitamin Sea.

Wednesday
DAY 212

Boundaries. These are so difficult for me to enforce, especially around alcohol (my mother's issue) and money (my father's issue). I tend to let it go when people turn into mean drunks and start saying horrible things to me.

What is that about?

I tend to love everyone when I'm pissed, so I don't really get the urge to be ugly to someone, but I've experienced a few people telling me some home truths that they clearly didn't have the balls to mention to me when they were sober.

Then the money issue. Because of my father's Scrooge-like tendencies, I have a horror of being thought of as mean, so I tend to go overboard, but that leads to some people[6] treating me like an ATM.

Confrontation about the slightest thing is scary to me, so I will do almost anything to avoid it. I just push all these feelings down, which is not healthy.

Nice bit of news is that our book trailer is fabulous. At least that's a bright spot in what feels like endless dreariness. Not helped by the endless dreariness of the weather.

Although, good to be gloomy while I have to work so hard. Just hope it warms up a bit and the sun comes out during my break.

Thursday
DAY 213

Beyond stressed.

Felt like I was honestly losing it yesterday.

Need to calm down.

Can only do what I can do.

I hate my Husband at the moment. He speaks to me in this low soothing voice as if I'm a wild animal.

Patronising AF.

Christ, do I really have to be grateful for anything this morning?

- Coffee
- Rain
- The end.

Friday
DAY 214

Biggest news today is that Marian loved our book (yes, we are on a first name basis *flicks hair*). Her generosity astounds me. Yesterday was the 25th anniversary of *Rachel's Holiday* being published, plus Marian

6 Especially the people I gave birth to.

was recording the audio for the sequel, *Again, Rachel,* and she STILL found the time to read our book and send Schim a reply. I mean . . . she is the absolute greatest of all time.

Hilarious bit was that I had terrible insomnia last night and the beginnings of a migraine, so I slept in until 7.30 and the girls were desperate to tell me the news. Schim was going to get her husband to phone my Husband. Amy was regretting that she was on her way to the Midlands and couldn't come and scream at my gate.

I promised the kids we'd crack the bottle of French champers if we got a positive response from Marian. But I feel uneasy about drinking now; it makes me feel weirdly guilty.

Saturday
DAY 215

So we opened the French champers and toasted all our various successes. The Firstborn has passed, the Lastborn got five As, Marian loved our book. I drank a full glass of champers, then I drank a half a glass, then a half of prosecco and then I kept having sips of the Husband's red wine – probably a half a glass? So maybe 2.5 to 3 glasses of alcohol altogether, which is a lot for me now.

I was fairly underwhelmed by the champers and the prosecco. The prosecco tastes very sweet. But the red wine was gorgeous. What I noticed is that I drink waaaaaay faster than the kids. I gulp mine down. But I got to a point where I felt merry and then I stopped and had water. The Firstborn was terribly sweet and said he thinks I don't drink nearly as much as my peers. Which might be true, but I suspect I can't handle it as well. I then went to bed and slept like a baby.

Think I kind of needed to let my hair down.

While all this was going on, we had beekeepers in getting rid of a swarm of bees that had taken up residence in our one air vent. It was the most bizarre evening.

This morning, when we stopped for coffee in Tyrone Avenue after picking up our Christmas tree, the key to the bloody car wouldn't work. We abandoned said car and I stomped off home in an absolutely foul mood. It was the literal straw that broke the camel's back. Apparently, the kids knew the key didn't work but didn't tell us. Grrrr. Also, the Husband was not being enormously helpful at the Christmas tree place, chatting to friends, not standing in the queue, leaving me to pay. I was not impressed.

I've been so stressed over work. Eventually, this show will consist of a series of one-way phone calls in sets that make no sense with whichever actors remain.

Nightmare on Elm Street.

I keep reiterating that I will not be available after the 15th. I hope everyone is taking that in.

Sunday
DAY 216

The anger has left me and now only sadness remains. I am so fucking sad; I just want to sit at my computer and weep. But I have to work.

Am feeling weighed down by sadness. Feel burdened by everything I have to pay for.

Feel burdened – by everything really.

The last two years of this pandemic have finished me.

Hope I do manage to have a bit of a break.

Cool, cloudy weather.

Vaal Dam climbed by ten per cent last week.

We are putting up the Christmas tree today.

The Husband has now gone shopping with the Lastborn for my Christmas present. I am mildly interested but mostly just don't give a shit. Hopefully, when I've had a break, I might be more filled with the Christmas spirit; at the moment, just sadness.

PS: Reading very dull Ron Howard memoir that is boring me to tears. He should've stuck to directing.

Monday
DAY 217

Watched v good Sandra Bullock movie on Netflix – *The Unforgivable*. But not sure what she's done to her face. Looks weird.

Reading fab piece of erotic fiction about an older woman who has a red-hot affair with a young pop star, called *The Idea of You* by Robinne Lee. It was recommended by a man on FB who referred to it as 'chick-lit'. Sigh.

Sadness still with me. Compounded by a mild panic that I won't get everything done before I leave.

Also, am feeling fat and old and ugly.

Think I'm anxious not knowing when I'm going to get work from shows 2 and 3 – not knowing if the peeps from Show 1 are going to sneakily try and send me work while I'm on leave.

It's all a bit damn much for one person.

Wednesday
DAY 219

Soooooo got scripts to write from shows 2 and 3 over my break, and eight scripts to edit from Show 2 when I get back from my break. I handed in my script for Show 3 and told them that I don't know if I'll be able to take another script over this festive season. That took enormous self-control as I find it almost impossible to turn down work. But I must have a break. I must or I might kill someone.

I wish I were kidding.

We leave tomorrow for the coast. Have checked the app and seen that the weather is shitty when we first get there and then improves. Will just be lovely to have a break.

Getting nails done at nine today.

Took family pic by the Christmas tree last night. The Lastborn was slightly grumpy but has brilliant acting skills so managed to look like she loved all of us.

We've organised a family braai at the coast on Sunday with the Husband's family and other old friends that we (shockingly) haven't seen for six years. Boxing Day lunch will be in Joburg with Little Brother and his fam. Should be nice.

No New Year's Eve plans yet. Cancelled our trip to the Cradle of Humankind, where we were going to spend a couple of nights in the hotel. Wasn't sure I was in the mood – also not in the mood to spend all that loot, especially after I paid for an extra night at the coast.

On the book front, not only did Marian love *Chasing Marian,* but Schim sent her the teaser and Marian then tweeted about it to her 300k followers. Feels like a bit of a dream. I then had this anxiety attack about posting the tweet. I think it just felt like shit was getting real and I wasn't ready. This all felt like it was happening to someone else.

Booze-wise, I am going to allow myself to drink on certain days over the festive season. Might have a drink with fam and friends on Sunday. But more likely to have one on Christmas Eve lunch, on Boxing Day with my fam and on New Year's Eve?

I drank last Friday, and I didn't have a craving to carry on drinking for the rest of the weekend, that was enough for me.

I know for sure that I am not in the same league as all the people in the books I have read. I don't have alcohol use disorder, but it is something I am going to have to watch for the rest of my life because it is a slippery slope for those of us who've grown up with alcoholics or who have a predisposition for it.

Do we all drink too much? For sure and I think the binge drinking is terrible, but I really don't think an occasional drink is a problem. I have friends that can and do drink like that. They can take it or leave it.

I think that this is the trickier option for not getting shitfaced but that it's probably the solution for me. If I cannot stick to it, then I'll have to revisit the idea of going completely dry.

Allowing myself specific days to drink and not drinking every day is most possibly the solution for me. Also, going to a pub and drinking a really appalling glass of red wine doesn't do it for me. I'd rather have a cup of coffee.

I have gone for seven months barely touching alcohol and I think

I needed that. I needed to kind of detox and take stock. Because of my family background, alcohol may well be something I wrestle with for the rest of my life. And that's okay. As long as I am always mindful of what I am doing.

My last blog for 2021:

Choose your story

I used to work with someone in the TV industry who insisted that his was the only way to tell the stories we were working on. He was a very talented individual, so it pains me to say this, dear Reader, but he was talking out of his bottom. There are many ways to tell a story. The same is true of our lives. I could tell a story of a country that made a huge blunder by announcing this new variant, which sadly I keep calling omnibus, or I could tell a story of a country that felt it was their ethical duty to report the new variant even though it would cost them dearly. I choose the second story and likewise I choose a story of hope this Christmas, and it was in this spirit that I decided to try and save my oak tree.

I have mentioned before the story of my oak tree on this blog but because I have Covidy-menopausal brain, I feel completely entitled to repeat myself (and to call the children by the cats' names just as my parents did before me.) What happened is this: an old man pitched up at our house when it was inhabited by the previous owners and said that the oak tree had been planted to celebrate his birth 80 years previously. Our oak tree turns 100 in 2024 but sadly, it is riddled with PSHB – the dastardly shot-hole borer. I had decided to release the whole issue to the universe and hope that my tree would fight the little bastards off and survive. But as it started losing more and more branches, I thought sod the releasing it to the universe story, did a little bit of research and came across some positive stories of companies that had been applying certain fungicides and pesticides and having results against the bastard beetle.

A lovely man called Johan from MHS Agricare came around to my house last week and had a look at my trees. He gave me a quote for the oak and for the viburnum and also identified a rather magnificent tree in my back garden as being a wild oak. We had a wonderful chat about forest bathing, and I did confess that I have taken to hugging my oak tree and (in the manner of a certain politician) telling the shot-hole borers to fuck off back from whence they came. Johan came and sprayed my tree this week and will be doing it again in a couple of weeks' time. Dear Reader, if this treatment doesn't work, I will be sad but not angry, because I know that I did my best to save my beloved oak. MHS Agricare are busy trying to save trees at Jeppe High School for Girls and in Melrose Arch and they know their shit, so do drop them a line if you have a tree you would like to try and save. I was sad to hear that our beloved jacaranda trees are now being infected. PSHB is much like Covid and just keeps getting cleverer.

Because of the new clever rona variant, my daughter's school was not able to do Interhouse Arts, which was rather devastating after the daughter had spent the weekend writing the script and sourcing the music. We also had to contact the family and cancel the Christmas lunch we had planned for December 11th. 'But I've already bought my dress for it,' wailed my sister.

Not seeing family is one of the hardest things about this shitshow. We were supposed to celebrate my sister's 60th birthday in Tuscany in 2020. We have put the trip off until 2023. Because of this, my sister has decided that she will only turn 60 then and our one brother, who used to be younger than her, will at that point be older. My son then announced in that case he would be staying 21 until we go to Tuscany, which means that my kids may well land up being twins. Like I said, choose your story and stick to it.

I am not a huge fan of Black Friday but the one thing I did take advantage of was the two-for-one sale at Lindt. I got lured in there last Saturday (not much luring was required) and purchased the calendars for my kids.

Shop Assistant: Ah ... how old are they?

Me: 17 and 21.

I am signing out now until 2022, so I would like to take this moment to thank all of you who have read and shared this blog. Merry Christmas to those who celebrate and my love to you all. Keep safe and happy reading.

xxx

JANUARY

Sunday
Day 237
Happy New Year!

I stuck to my guns and did not look at any work stuff for the two weeks I was off. Okay, I'm lying a smidge. I did submit a quick script on Friday, 17 December, but after that, I did sweet FA. So I've had a lovely break and am defs feeling more relaxed than I did two weeks ago.

Officially this is the first day of work for me. Have a script to write for Show 3 by the end of Monday. I'm relieved as I spent an absolute fortune on this break. The holiday to the coast set me back far too much and I had the depressing realisation that we could've had four nights in a really fancy hotel, with three meals a day and everything laid on, for what I spent.

My holiday in point form:

- ✔ Got a flight on the 16th to KZN – flight was scarily empty for a public holiday and the beginning of the holidays in SA.
- ✔ The kids promptly had mimosas in the Slow Lounge. I had coffee. Was sooooooo lovely to be at the airport going somewhere. And the Slow Lounge. I lurrrrve the SL, even though they didn't have my fave choccie croissants and everything is wrapped in cellophane because of the rona.

- ✔ Storming when we left so quite a bumpy flight, but I had my Headspace Fear of Flying meditation and was fine.
- ✔ It was creepy seeing the burnt-out factory as we headed off to the South Coast from King Shaka International Airport.
- ✔ Unlike the Western Cape, KZN defs felt quiet – a combo of Covid and the riots. Everyone wearing masks and being careful.
- ✔ Our holiday home looked the same as when we stayed there in 2013/14 except that they had redone the kitchen. We were sad that there's no longer a gate to the dune in front of the house. It was such a lovely place for sundowners, and the kids used their bodyboards to surf down the dunes the last time we were here. The owners also mentioned that they're putting in their papers for the US. Plus, they are putting their faith in Ivermectin. Oh-kay.

- ✻ Pizzas from our fave pizza place on the first night were not that nice, apparently because the original owner died, which we thought was excessively inconsiderate of him.
- ✻ Crappy weather the first day and a bite but we went to Shelly Centre and bought half of Woolies. Again – shopping centre was not that busy. Staff were so nice.
- ✻ The weather improved and we managed to spend every day on the beach. The sea was perfect for me, but no nice waves for the others until the last day. But hey, at least Mama was happy.
- ✻ Lovely family do with the Husband's family, whom we haven't seen for six years, and with old friends. Bryn doesn't really drink anymore so we had a good chat about that. His wife and kids are lovely, and also don't drink much.
- ✻ The Lastborn was sucking down the gins like water, which made me a bit anxious.
- ✻ The Firstborn kept telling me how bored he was and how he would rather be in St Francis or Plett. Truth is, we would've got a broom cupboard in Plett for what we paid for our holiday home on the South Coast. I didn't say that, just told him

that since he's now an adult, he doesn't have to come on holidays with us anymore. He promptly shut up after that.

* He had a virtual grad ceremony that we watched on TV. Not the same.

Came back home and immediately went into frenzied Christmas shopping mode. Big party on the 23rd. Everyone got roaring drunk in the family except for me. It was a karaoke do and both the offspring were holding on to the mic with a white-knuckle death grip and the Firstborn was also very attached to a bottle of tequila. Luckily, they both have very good voices but still I was mortified. Because guess who they reminded me of? ME!!

The offspring and Husband had horrible hangovers and we then headed to a friend for Christmas Eve lunch. The Firstborn had to have a lie-down, he was feeling so terrible. I drank a small glass of eggnog and a glass and a half of red wine and felt ill. Luckily, it wore off by the evening.

Quiet Christmas with just us, which was lovely. Bought the kids a dartboard and a whole lot of clothes, which were a huge hit.

Boxing Day we had my family around and it was very special to see my very, very clever nephew who is now based in the UK and doing a PhD in maths. Drank a glass of red wine: made my heart race and generally made me feel weird. Bit sad, that. My nephew didn't want to go home, and I have to admit, I did get a bit tired. Sands, who barely drinks because of her multiple sclerosis, is a great inspiration to me. She's not a party pooper and is always the designated driver but still will have one or two gins.

Discovery Vitality check. Cholesterol is five – a point down from last year, but still not good enough. Hmm.

We were invited out for NYE but chose to stay at home – just the two of us. It was perfect. I bought some crème de cassis and thought I would top it up with dealc'd champers to make a semi-alcoholic kir royale – but it didn't really taste the same. Will make it a bit stronger today and see what it tastes like.

The Lastborn is now in Cape Town, spending all her Christmas money.

I do worry about her drinking. But I realise she is now an adult and I have to let her make her own mistakes – within reason.

Cleaning up vomit from the offspring after the all-fall-down Christmas party was a bit of an eye-opener for me. It made me realise that my not-drinking is not going to magically make the kids not drink. That what might be a better example for them is me having a couple of drinks and saying, 'Thanks, but I've had enough.'

However, do not quote me on this. The thing about parenting is that none of us actually know what we're doing. We do what we can and then hope like hell our kids will be okay. People who tell you differently are lying or are in for a rude shock when things don't work out as planned.

The vomming also took me back to a similar event when I was at university. I got one of the main parts in the third-year play – the stepdaughter in *Six Characters in Search of an Author*. Incidentally, the play is where I first got together with the Husband. During the rehearsal period, I went out with a bunch of friends for what I think was a 21st-birthday dinner. I got slammed, woke up in the middle of the night, sat up and puked red wine all over my duvet and got some in my hair (truly gorgeous). I called my mother, who washed and dried my hair for me, changed the bedding and put me back to bed.

I told the director of the play I had gastro.

My mother agreed that I had gastro.

Reader, I did not have gastro.

I never want to pretend with the offspring. If I am drunk, we will call it what it is, same goes for them.

In this spirit of honesty I have to say that this was quite a boozy holiday season for me (). This is the tally:

* 1.75 glasses of champers on Fri night
* 1 glass cheap red wine at trailer-trashy restaurant (soooooo many old-style mullets, not the funky new variety)
* 1 glass champers on Monday night – did not enjoy it
* I glass red wine at Bidvest airport lounge – nice!
* 1 glass eggnog, 1.5 glasses of red wine on Christmas Eve – felt ill
* 1 glass red wine on Boxing Day – had had lunch, sipped it slowly – still gave me a headache.

Not sure whether to count the crème de cassis as I had hardly any?

Funny thing is, I just started drinking the dealc'd champers on its own and preferred it to the kir royale.

I notice that my skin was itchy as hell when I got back from the coast – partly sun allergy but also booze, I suspect, and my heels started cracking. Must add, I do not enjoy the heart-racing thing I feel when I start drinking the red wine.

I don't have any answers as to whether I should give up or not. I feel incredibly proud for having given myself a chance to re-evaluate everything. I have loved these almost eight months of not being drunk and not having a hangover

I still maintain that alcohol is an anaesthetic that keeps us from living our lives to the fullest. And, if I'm honest, the only reason I drank these holidays was to feel a sense of belonging. So perhaps my next year will be no booze at all?

Am a bit of a porky pig.

Weight: 71.4 kg

Not brilliant. But obvs have been stuffing my face festively so hopefully I will lose weight quite quickly. Dare not say anything about being fat in front of the Lastborn. She is an avenging angel in terms of body positivity and will make me do affirmations in front of the mirror if I say anything negative about myself. I do love this about her and her generation.

Monday
DAY 238

Back at work on Show 1 today. Was so tired after writing the script for Show 3 yesterday that I went to sleep at 10 pm. Woke up at six.

My New Year's resolutions usually have to do with work goals, but this year, they centre around self-care. It's a first for me.

- ✔ Make time for exercise
- ✔ Meditate more
- ✔ Save money

- ✔ Say no
- ✔ Continue sober curiosity
- ✔ Finish memoir
- ✔ Exercise compassion
- ✔ Have medical check-ups
- ✔ Find the grey. (Not the grey hairs. They're not easy to miss.) Find the grey means learn to walk in the middle of the road and don't be tempted to see everything in black and white.
- ✔ LAUGH MORE!

So that's it. Have already signed up for the Stash app to try and save a bit of money so have made a start.

Big storm last night, so beautiful morning. World looks washed clean.

Tuesday
DAY 239

I am inching towards that first-year anniversary of being sober curious. Every time I say the words *sober curious* it makes the son crack up. Although I'm kind of confused about where I fit in on the drinking spectrum, the summary of my year of trying this out are: I have never had more than three drinks in a sitting, have not got shitfaced and have not had a hangover. That is a brilliant feeling for someone who drank too much every weekend.

SA Parliament is on fire. Arson – a sign of the general unrest that is happening around the world. I still cannot believe we have lived through a pandemic. I have lost so many colleagues and friends and I haven't really processed it yet. I have this sense of not allowing myself to be too happy about anything . . . kind of waiting for the other shoe to drop.

This omicron variant is milder but more contagious – lots of infections but way fewer deaths. Please God this is the end of the pandemic.

Saw an interesting thing on TikTok about growing up with an unreliable caregiver – like an alcoholic, for example – and fawning. Fawning is basically people-pleasing. Really hit home because I know that I fawn – and am desperate for people to like me.

Okay, before you start imagining that I was locked in a cupboard for three years as a child and regularly beaten and now have dissociative identity disorder (what used to be multiple personality disorder. Think of the movie *Sybil*), let me assure you this was not the case. We did have that thing where my mother threw her slipper at us, and you had to bring it back for a hiding but that happened to everyone. It was more the fighting in the house, my mother's drinking, my father's verbal cruelty and the biggie, which was living through a war (the Zimbabwean War of Liberation). I can remember always being scared:

Exhibit A

We are travelling to South Africa from what was then Rhodesia for our annual holiday. I think it's in December and I must be eight or nine because Big Brother, who is ten years older than me, is in the Rhodesian army. We miss the convoy, which leaves without us. We travel with my brother's rifle sticking out the window to frighten off any terrs (terrorists). I am terrified. On the way home from South Africa we make sure we catch the convoy. The instructions are that if we are fired on, we have to stop the car, open the doors and roll out into the ditch. I don't feel reassured.

Exhibit B

It is, quite literally, a dark and stormy night. There is a car idling at the top of our driveway in Salisbury (now Harare). My father goes to see who it is. The man who works for us is sitting in the passenger seat of a car driven by an old white man. The white man pulls out a gun and holds it to the head of the black man. Nothing happens. We find out later the white man wanted to mentally torture the black man.

Exhibit C

We are flying to South Africa to go overseas. The lights in the plane have to be switched off in case the terrs see us and shoot us down. This is after two planes were shot down and the survivors were gunned down. I can remember holding my breath until we crossed into South African airspace and the lights were switched back on.

We were furiously and patriotically Rhodesian. I knew all the words to the national anthem and 'Rhodesians Never Die' and thought Robert Mugabe was the devil incarnate.

I only realised when I arrived in South Africa and attended the very progressive Sacred Heart College that we were on the wrong side.

Living through that as a young kid who didn't really know what was going on was enough to make me want to escape from reality.

I first got the sense that there was something wrong with me when I was about ten. Perhaps I was younger. We were living in our house in Salisbury. I didn't feel real. I would look at myself in the mirror and try to come back to myself by repeating, 'I am Pamela Power.' I would say this over and over, until I had the sense of coming back to the present, coming back to my body, and becoming aware that I was in fact real.

I found out later from my lovely therapist, Judith Ancer, that this was a mild form of dissociation called depersonalisation disorder. It was such a relief to find out I wasn't nuts (well, not completely). The psychological thriller I've been working on forever is about this. As always, it was only later it occurred to me that writing about it was me trying to make sense of my own dissociative disorder.

The Husband started running this morning, which nearly killed him. I did weights, which nearly killed me. I'm sure he will have dropped weight by the end of the week. We both will. If we don't die first.

The Lastborn is still in CT. Am really missing her. Dreading her going to varsity next year.

Wednesday
DAY 240

Reasonably good night's sleep last night. The Husband's alarm woke us at 6.30. Did two sets of 15 squats and heel raises and yoga stretches and meditation. Am trying to be disciplined about this.

Work is insane, with everyone wanting scripts yesterday. Very proud that I managed to tell Goneril from Show 2 that I could not submit the scripts by Thursday. Will be working the whole weekend but then things should calm down.

The Husband has the possibility of staying on after his contract ends – I really hope this comes off – plus business does seem to be picking up at Go See Do, so it's all quite promising.

I will have been working on soapies for 20 years by the end of this year. I started on *Generations* in 2003.

And this is the Lastborn's final year of school.

Plus, it is the ten-year anniversary of when I was first digitally published.

I have achieved stuff that I never thought I would. My 'wildest dreams' achievement would have been 'international bestselling novelist', but I suspect that even if that had been achieved, I still wouldn't think I was good enough.

Next year I will have been married for 30 years and we will have been together for 35. That is a long time.

This is a time of milestones.

Beautiful sunny days and rain at night. Such perfect weather.

Thursday
DAY 241

This would be the day we usually would take the Christmas tree down, but I have too much work, so I suspect it'll only happen on the weekend. Also, I loathe taking the tree down. It means Christmas – my best time of the year – is over. Frankly, would just keep it up the whole year if I could.

The Lastborn got home last night brimming with stories from CT. Think she had a blast but now it's time to come back down to earth and get on with the year.

The Firstborn is at a loose end, hasn't heard back from the universities about Honours and is not particularly interested. Just wants to go and travel and I get that.

Hopefully this contract extension happens for the Husband. Fingers crossed.

As always, there's my constant underlying anxiety that I will continue to have work.

That's why I want Go See Do to work so that we always have a back-up. I'm tired of living from hand to mouth.

My meditation this morning was about how everything changes, nothing stays the same – including our shitty financial state. It can improve.

Got invited to sundowners this evening. But, alas, I'm too busy. I say alas, I am alarmingly happy to eat wine gums in front of Netflix these days.

PSA: wine gums do not contain wine.

Friday
DAY 242

Godson Jay's birthday today.

Twelve years ago, in the middle of the Soccer World Cup and just six weeks after my mother died, he was found lying face down in a pool of blood in Lusaka and had to be medevac'd to Joburg. He had a terrible case of malaria, was in a coma with multi-organ failure for nine days and had nine toes amputated as a result. He's now married to a lovely Welsh woman and has two adorable kids. Wearing flip-flops, however, is out for him.

My weight was down to 70 on the nail this morning – 1.4 lower than Monday. Diets work. Intermittent fasting, done properly, works.

Admittedly, I had also had two wees and a poo and taken all my kit off.

But still.

Have also exercised this week. Religiously. Every morning. 2 x arms, 2 x tummy, 1 x legs. Plus walked just about every day. But I know it's the diet that does the trick. It's all about what you put in your mouth.

Blah weather at the mo' – 19 degrees and rainy yesterday. Ugh.

Just read journal from a year ago. Was soooooo bleak. The Husband was earning zip, I was still sick as a dog with the rona, offspring had had a beyond-shitty Christmas. Feel so grateful that the beginning of this year feels different and that I've had a two-week break.

What a difference a year makes!

Saturday
DAY 243

Went to Red Wine Friday last night. Drank fake champagne and had a cup of tea and was ready to come home by 9.30 pm. Lovely to see everyone, but if you take wine out of the equation, so much of our socialising seems utterly pointless. I am much happier being at home, watching a movie or reading a book or writing. Although one of the young people there did tell me I had amazing skin.

Sobriety? Or the shimmer powder from the Body Shop?

Went into an absolute spiral yesterday afternoon because I read that someone was invited to a workshop for Show 2 and I wasn't. Then went and reread the head writer's letter from Show 3 saying that they would be bringing in new writers for the new season and started shitting off. This triggers some of my worst fears: that I have been left behind; that I will never work again.

I've been working in this industry for 19 years and I still have these moments. Keep feeling frantic at the thought of being cut from two of the shows I work on simultaneously.

Now feeling terrible that I spent so much money on our holiday.

Was also sent notes by the new head writer on Show 1 that set me off. Immediate thoughts:

- ✔ I haven't even been paid for last month's work – how very dare they?
- ✔ Does this person not realise how much rewriting I've already done on these scripts?
- ✔ How dare they criticise the previous head writer's work?

I don't think the head writer in question had an inkling of how much the email pissed me off. The good thing is that I took a deep breath and responded – disagreeing with some of the comments. But it made me feel like shite.

Usually, I would've dived into a glass of prosecco followed shortly by several glasses of red wine to deal with my feelings of discomfort. Now I just have to deal with them. The only way out is through.

Also, a favourite trick of mine would be to go behind someone's back and moan to their superior (or really anyone who would listen) about them. I've been trying for a while now not to be that asshole, to deal with issues directly instead.

Sunday
DAY 244

Just realised that I've never done a January without grog before. God.

Had a good chat with the Husband yesterday about what I do enjoy doing besides going to the pub. I thought about it and things I've enjoyed included:

- Schim's book launch
- Christmas lunch with the Husband's fam and our old friends
- Christmas Eve lunch with Red Wine Friday friends
- Boxing Day with my fam
- Coffee and sitting in the park
- Movies with my kids
- Days on the beach
- Fournos for coffee and croissants.

But mostly staying at home, writing, reading, watching TV, lying in the garden and swimming.

Giving up drinking is like being on a diet: you need to find things to replace your old habits.

One thing I was very proud of is that I reversed out of the driveway and drove home on Friday night and told the Husband to STFU when he tried to tell me where I should be driving. The more you do the uncomfortable things, the more comfortable you will become with them.

I exercised five days last week and went for a walk yesterday even though I was beyond sleep-deprived.

Cloudy, rainy weather. Pool is filled to overflowing.

Still the odd jacaranda blossom around.
Yesterday, today and tomorrow has a few blooms on it.
Oak tree's had its third jab.
Roses are not enjoying all the rain. They need some sun.

Later: am now feeling a lot more chipper. Maybe because I've handed in my script edits for Show 2? Who knows? Maybe it's the caffeine? Just feel lighter and more hopeful . . . like something cool is about to happen . . .

Tuesday
DAY 246

The Husband drank a bottle of red wine on Sunday night, then snored all night and woke me up. Grrrr.

Other people's drinking is not my concern. Other people's drinking is not my concern. Other people's drinking is not my concern. Other people's drinking is not my concern. Other people's drinking is not my concern. Other people's drinking is not my concern.

Just about every quitlit book I've read has said this. Do not think you are an Apostle of Sobriety and you have to spread the gospel to everyone like an irritating Seventh-Day Adventist. Learn to STFU.

Having said that, I have noticed how drunk people are either over-sentimental or over-emotional or loud or just plain mean. Once you've opened your eyes to what alcohol does to people, you cannot go back. I wish that I could just go back to drinking like everyone else, but those days are gone for me.

I miss getting tanked, all the silliness and exuberance that goes with it. But I don't miss anything else about it. I also know that if I just carry on socialising sober, I will eventually get my mojo back and be as exuberant as ever. I've already had flashes of it.

Uncle Kenny (remember my recovered alkie uncle?) was sober for as long as I knew him. He would sit at family gatherings with a cup of tea, chuckling and shaking his head at the family's drunken antics. Apparently, he had been a nightmare drunk back in the day, but I only knew the sober version and he was lovely. I travelled up to Harare with him and Auntie Ray for my sister's wedding. Auntie Ray and I slept in the same bed when we moved down to Joburg together. I named the Lastborn after her.

Went to a first meeting for the Lastborn's matric dance dress. Think it's going to be beautiful. Went to all these bridal shops at the mall to try and find her something. Nearly passed out when I found out the prices, and for these terrible be-sequinned, be-dazzled numbers. Was thrilled to get the contact deets for dress designer, Nadia Kruger, a film and theatre contact from writer Ros Butler. Nadia knows all the same people I know, so we ended up having a fabulous chinwag and she won't charge me a fortune.

Still haven't been paid by Show 1. Hopefully by Thursday. Still don't know if my contract will be renewed by Show 3. Sigh. Show 2 I'm slightly more hopeful about, but who knows?

Wednesday
DAY 247

Got paid last night. Tralalalala!!

But one of the producers on Show 1 called me and told me that they can't be sure that they're going to get the money for the next ten episodes so I effectively stop work on Tues. Part of me felt panicky and the other part felt relieved because tomorrow we have the cover and title reveal for *Chasing Marian* and next Wednesday is the Lastborn's 18th birthday.

That's all over and above the fact that I had a migraine yesterday and have carpal tunnel pain from typing so much (yes, and from scrolling on my phone), so a little breather here might be very welcome. Also, these are very lovely people who I can tell are in agonies about paying people late. As an employer myself, I sympathise.

The Lastborn is stressed to the max and upset because they can't do war cries at the interhouse gala due to Covid. The Firstborn finds out next week if he got into Honours. He doesn't seem enormously keen.

Weather still crap. Had a god-almighty thunderstorm yesterday. Came down in buckets!

Friday
DAY 249

The cover reveal ended up happening three hours late but was a dream come true – especially because Marian tweeted about it last night. So that's pretty huge. Now we have to wait and see if we get a UK deal out of it.

Am not feeling great at the moment. Queasy and headachy. Not sure WTF is going on. Maybe stress? Covid?

Weight: got on the scale this morning: 70.1 but after a coffee and water.

Picked up the pearls I ordered for the Lastborn's birthday. They are stunning! Very chuffed with them.

Monday
DAY 252

Tried some low-alcohol red wine over the weekend. A third of the alcohol of normal red wine.

Positives: did not make me feel pissed at all.

Negatives: Tasted like cat's pee.

Suspect the white wine would taste better – or maybe a blend? Going to experiment with it. Would also love to get hold of a low-alcohol sparkling wine.

Had the realisation that moderation and fence-sitting is what I'm all about. Flexitarian rather than vegetarian, sober curious rather than sober. The grey in the middle of the black and white is where I sit. I learnt all about taking the middle road from Ailsa Frank's self-hypnosis. She has fabulous ones to help you cut down the drinking and from her book *Cut the Crap and Feel Amazing* which I found very useful.

Fantastic interview with Sara-Jayne Makwala on CapeTalk about *Chasing Marian*. We're having a lot of fun with it already.

Quite a big upset over the weekend because I was planning the Lastborn's 18th birthday party and then she told me her friends had planned a surprise party for her on Friday. I vetoed the Friday-night thing because she has a huge swimming gala on Saturday morning and is swimming captain. So, guess whose party got axed? Mine.

Realisation last night after spending far too long on TikTok. Came across a post that said something to the effect of 'your parents didn't go out of their way to make your life shit, they just didn't know any better'. Made me feel so much better. Also, my kids' behaviour towards me is now giving me a lot of sympathy for my mom and how I dismissed her and made her feel bad. Karma is a bitch.

It made me think about Dad too– was his meanness a reaction to Evie, who wouldn't or couldn't get a job? Had he had enough of her drinking and that made him behave like that? Also, at the end of his life, he was getting smashed at parties. Had he given up?

Felt a lot of empathy for him suddenly.

God, I might finally be growing up!

Thursday
DAY 255

Daughter's 18th birthday yesterday. We went to a restaurant called Lucé at the Hyde Park Hotel because it reminded us of the Husband's late mum (her name was Lucia.) Food was so-so, view was fantastic and waiter was hilarious. There was absolutely no one there when we arrived, not even the music was playing, so I asked the waiter if we had scared everyone away.

Him: I was thinking the same thing.

Luckily, more people arrived later on.

I had a glass of sparkling wine and a glass of red wine accompanied by a bottle of Pellegrino. I think this is the way forward for me. I felt mellow but not drunk I felt like I was taking part in the libations, but we weren't going overboard. The Firstborn wanted a third cocktail. I said no, we needed to go home, so the Lastborn gave him hers. The Husband had two and a half beers (not that anyone's counting.)

Other people's drinking is none of my business.

It was a really lovely evening.

Sunday
DAY 258

Everyone went out on Saturday night – the Firstborn to friends, the Husband to a school reunion and the Lastborn to her 18th birthday party held at a friend's house. I thought that perhaps I would have a delicious glass of red wine with a pizza for dinner and then decided, 'Nah, what for?'

Also, I'd been watching vids on TikTok from this shrink that talks about how any amount of booze shrinks the brain, so that gave me the heebies. Really don't want to lose the three brain cells I still have.

I did wonder if the Lastborn wanted to have her birthday party at the friend's house because I wouldn't be drinking and would be keeping my eagle eye on her? But the friend's mother doesn't drink either . . . hmmm.

I had a horrible upset tummy, which I think is because I am stressed about work and the lack thereof. Also stress about the Lastborn excluding us from her birthday party – we got to pay for it but we weren't invited.

I can no longer self-medicate so I just had to wade through all the unpleasant feelings. Ho hum. Not easy.

Got a horrible hollow feeling when I saw today on Twitter that another writer colleague is now writing on Show 2. Can't help wondering if they wanted to see my contract so that they could schny/schnie me (have no idea how to spell that.[7])

Oh well. I release it to the universe.

Monday
DAY 259

Final, final edits on *Chasing Marian*. Still fretting about what other work I will have (if any!).

7 Editor tells me it is probably 'schnaai', a uniquely South African mash-up using a Yiddish or German-sounding consonant blend at the beginning and rounded off with the Afrikaans word 'naai', a richly evocative swearword that emerged from the Afrikaans word for 'sew'.

My dream would be to work on Show 1 and work on novels (and get paid for it). I really don't want to work on so many shows at once, it's just that I need the money. I feel like Hugh Hefner with his three young girlfriends, except I can't just pop a little blue pill to get it up. Would be fab if Go See Do paid me and I got to work on some dramas/sitcoms (hint, hint, hint).

Have had a couple of weeks of shitty weather but it's supposed to get hot in the middle of the week. God, I cannot wait!!

Some peeps have left the WhatsApp group for Show 2, which kind of confirms that I didn't make the cut, which is rather upsetting. The most upsetting part is that they didn't even have the balls to tell me. But it is what it is. I also cannot kick up a fuss because it means I might never get work with them again and I can't afford to do that.

On the other hand, it makes me more convinced than ever that I don't want to work with people who treat me like this.

I approach the future with curiosity.

Wednesday
DAY 261

Yesterday was a bit of a shitshow. I emailed the former head writer of Show 3 and asked her if she knew what was going on. She told me that she heard that the new head writer had already had a meeting with his new team. Ergo, I could only presume that I had been axed. Cue panic stations. How the hell could I be axed from Show 2 and Show 3 in the same month?? Arghhhhhhhhh! Felt like I was having an anxiety attack. Immediately emailed all my contacts about a side gig. Then got a weird contract addendum from Show 3 extending my contract until April.

So I am still working for Show 3.

I have definitely been cut from Show 2. Still cannot believe that I've been axed from a show I've worked on for so many years without even a goodbye. Fuckers!

And here's the weird thing: if they need me in six months' time, I will just get an email out of the blue as if nothing had happened.

In happier news, *Chasing Marian* is now available for pre-order on Amazon and even has a sales ranking, which means people are buying it! We are still waiting to hear if we have an overseas deal.

On the Covid front, restrictions are easing up as the omicron wave subsides, and I hope we're heading to an endemic phase. I've had enough of the pandemic. We all have.

I am toing and froing over whether I should go completely sober, and I still believe the answer is no. I read somewhere that three drinks a week is probably optimal – that is not much considering I was in the 14–20 drinks range.

The Lastborn had a marimba event over the weekend cancelled because someone has Covid, and she is beyond irritated about it.

They just announced that there will be no liquor sold at the quiz night this Friday at the school, and everyone is up in arms.

I used to be that parent. I didn't want to go anywhere unless there was booze.

I can remember a family event. It was my cousin's child's First Communion. The church was packed, and we were beyond bored because the priest was droning on and on and on and there were about eleventy-twelve million kids making their communion. So we decided to all sneak out and drive around until we found a pub that was open. We went to the pub during the church service and arrived at the lunch afterwards already a bit smashed. This was not unusual behaviour in our family.

Another memory: a friend's wedding at a beautiful country hotel. The only drink there was the bottle of whisky on the rabbi's table. We left the wedding and went off and ordered drinks at the bar and moaned loudly about the lack of alcohol at the wedding.

What a selfish person I was. The only way I can comfort myself is to keep thinking, *when we know better, we do better*. (Please God, that I may or may not believe in, let me be better.)

The Husband will find out this week if they're extending his contract. The Firstborn is super-grumpy because his future is so uncertain, while the Husband and the Lastborn are still not speaking after the party debacle over the weekend. This upsets me because the Lastborn is a complete daddy's girl and they are usually so close. I have to steel myself not to interfere and to let them work through this. They are both champion sulkers, whereas the Firstborn and I are shouty door-slammers, which means this Cold War could go on for a while.

Family life is a bit fraught at the moment.

Friday
DAY 263

Moderation is all very well, but drinking just doesn't seem to agree with me anymore. Have no tolerance for it. Took a bottle of supposedly light fizzy wine to a writer friend yesterday to toast her new house and felt completely tipsy after one glass. Had about an inch more of the stuff and felt positively ill. So never mind me giving up booze, I think booze is giving up on me. Or maybe it's particularly cheap booze? Go, Princess Pammy! Battled to sleep last night and am now feeling shattered.

Also was nervous for PTA meeting this morning. Still have PTSD from the ones at the Firstborn's prep school. Now I'm at the end of my school journey with my kids, I'm a lot older and wilier and volunteer for nothing! They are also such a lovely bunch at the daughter's school, and the racial integration since I started on the PTA in 2006 – 16 years ago – is amazing.

Seems the Husband has had a bit of a reprieve and he is now being kept on as a consultant, so that's a relief. He won't be earning as much as he was previously so will have to top up cash from somewhere. Anyhoo, he does have money in his credit card for emergencies if we need it.

We are having a lot of fun with the novel. We're getting T-shirts made and everything. Launch on March 15th. All very exciting.

Supposed to be hot today but weather is incredibly blah.

Sunday
DAY 265

Very excited to see that Proud Mary in Rosebank stocks deacl'd champers and non-alcoholic gins. It's lovely that the restaurants are getting into this. Went there yesterday and had a cappuccino and a glass of Allure while the Husband had two beers. I didn't feel left out at all.

Still very worried about work and what's going to happen next. I saw a bunch of people outside churches this morning during our walk, which means that the churches have reopened and the pandemic is easing. But I think we're still carrying around a lot of trauma from the rona. I read my blog post from a year ago where I was recovering from Beta and my cousin had just lost his thirty-something son to Covid. It all feels like a bad dream.

The world feels like a profoundly changed place.

Meditation today on reframing the dreaded 'What if' to give it a positive spin.

'What if things actually do turn out?'

'What if *Chasing Marian* gets an overseas deal?'

'What if Go See Do starts raking in the cash?'

Approaching the future with optimism!

Shitty weather this weekend. Endless rain. Ugh.

PS: We have not been invited to the Franschhoek Literary Festival with *Chasing Marian*. Don't feel devastated – have been three times already so mustn't be greedy.

FEBRUARY

Tuesday
DAY 267

First day of February and I'm feeling upbeat. There's no money in the company that's employing the Husband at the moment so he might not have work after Feb, but I just approach the future with a what-if-everything-does-work-out attitude, as per new meditation.

Finally, we've had a respite from the rain, thanks god.

My weight went down to 69.8 last Friday. Okay, okay, maybe I did stand on one leg and lean against the wall to get it there, but at least it's dropped below 70.

This smartwatch I got with my new phone is really making me exercise. God, I do love a freebie! I was due a new phone at the end of December. In the past we have given our new phones to the offspring, especially when we couldn't afford decent presents for them at Christmas, but this year I needed a new one as the phone was starting to give up the ghost and the watch happened to be an added bonus. The Husband said he was happy to keep his old phone and kindly gave his new phone to the daughter, who had her phone stolen just before lockdown two years ago.

She was mugged outside the Service Station in Melville after getting her hair done. The guy snatched the phone out of her hand and then jumped into a waiting car. She ran after the car and jumped on the back of it, banging on the roof. The car roared away through the intersection. She chased it through the traffic. A man stopped and gave her a lift home. Yes, she got into a car with a man she did not know. I still break out in a cold sweat when I think of how that story could've ended.

Went for a walk by myself this morning and did tummy and yoga stretching/meditation. All good.

Thursday
DAY 269

When I say '69', the Husband still leers and raises an eyebrow which makes me larf. Marry someone who makes you laugh. The kids think we're beyond lame, but we still find each other funny.

Swam this morning because the weather was so gorgeous. Temps go down a little bit tomorrow and then crash over the weekend because there's some cyclone or something over Madagascar.

Friday
DAY 270

Am quickly writing a script today. Must be done by 2 pm.

Have loadshedding from 10 to 12.30.

Hahahaha!

But I know that Marian Keyes also has ridiculous deadlines. It doesn't stop just 'cause you're massively rich and famous.

Can you tell that I'm preparing to be massively rich and famous? I think I will be exceptionally good at it. Just putting that out there.

Do wonder how I would feel though if all money concerns were suddenly taken away from me. If I got a big fat advance for something. Think I wouldn't know what to do with myself because I'm so used to living like this.

Big storm brewing. Perfect weather to work in.

Saturday
DAY 271

Slept really well last night. The Lastborn's matric dance dress is looking beautiful and is nearly ready. It is a fitted, strapless, red satin gown with long red satin gloves, very old-world Hollywood.

Got my script in. Had a nice evening and woke up early. Lastborn didn't want to go to swimming – too exhausted – so we went for a walk and then had coffee and banana bread at Croft & Co. We went and did a practice run for her hair at the salon. Found shoes, bag and a fur stole at Rosebank, plus got make-up and hair clips. Nearly there. A few friends and some fam are coming to see her in her finery next weekend.

I see a lot of chuntering on social media about how over-the-top these matric dances are, but personally after being denied these special moments due to the rona, I'm totally here for all of the primping. I know of one of the Lastborn's friends who is spending 50k on her outfit and I can guarantee you right now no one will know the difference between that and the Lastborn's dress. It honestly does not worry me how much people spend and what cars they hire. I constantly preach to the kids that there will always be someone younger and prettier and richer and blah blah blah than you. Just do you and be happy with what you've got.

Bumped into the Firstborn's prep school music teacher at Blind Tiger – she has a friend who places kids as stooges (assistants) at private schools in the UK. Hoping she will find something for the Firstborn, who spends his time arguing with us and playing on his computer and watching YouTube videos. Yes, he's really using that BSc degree.

Rich son-in-law-to-be, hellooooooooo, where are you??

Monday
DAY 273

Went to Proud Mary. Had a glass of Allure – very nice – and a Duchess G&T – meh. Forgot to drink the white JC Le Roux. It's so hard to even want to drink once you've taken your blinkers off. I want to go back to the time before I knew what I know now.

I miss that moment of euphoria, though, when I could forget all my troubles, not be anxious, and also be looked after because I wouldn't have to drive home.

I'll probably have nostalgia for that feeling forever.

Last push to get final episodes in this week. In May, I will have been working for two years on Show 1, and because of Covid, I still haven't met some of the people. Crazy!!

Beautiful sunny day today. Leaves already starting to turn, which is slightly off-pissing. For two years we have had almost no summer because of La Niña.

Amazed that Go See Do actually made some money last year. Do not know how that happened. Obviously it all went to pay staff and we got none of it, but still, it's encouraging. Will be very exciting if more money comes in this year. Am starting to see some light at the end of the tunnel.

Found out from one of the other writers on Show 2 that the first breakdowns of the scripts went out last week, which means that I have most certainly been dropped. (Breakdowns, dear Reader, are essentially a plan of the episode. They are sent to the scriptwriters who then use them to write the script.) Very weird that I haven't been sent a Dear John letter. Might be keeping me around in case they need me or possibly just scared I'm going to sue them.

Still hurts and I feel anxious about the future.

Tuesday
DAY 274

Sadness. So much sadness. Feeling like a failure. Feeling like I'm a useless parent because I don't earn enough. Just wretched at the thought of all the work I did over November and December and January for Show 2 and this is how they treat me.

Wondering if I brought this all on myself.

Want to curl up in a ball and cry but can't. Have a pile of scripts to get through.

The only thing I try and hold on to is the idea that it's always darkest before dawn. That so many people gave up when they were just about to make it. Probably delusional but we all need hope.

It's all I have at this point.

Things I am grieving:

- Loss of financial security
- Being fat
- Kids who treat me like an ATM
- That I can't enjoy our book being launched 'cause everything's so shitty
- That I never even got thanked for everything I did for Show 2.

I am SAD, SAD, SAD.

Thursday
DAY 276

Woolies have a 'light' MCC champers – only nine per cent and lower in calories – so I'm going to try it on Saturday. Normal champers is 12 per cent, prosecco is 11 and vino is 14 or 15 per cent, so it is quite a bit of a difference.

I keep reading all this stuff about booze being carcinogenic. Here's the thing, though: you cannot protect yourself from everything in this world. I know that from personal experience. The Husband's nephew died of cancer just before he turned 11. Did he drink too much? Um . . . no. His parents were told he had the best cancer possible, really curable. Hmmm. He was diagnosed when the Firstborn was a month old and passed away when he was nine months. It was on my parents' wedding anniversary. He was also one of the Firstborn's godparents and adored him. For months after he died, the Firstborn would gaze into the distance at something only he could see and laugh delightedly.

When my father died, the Firstborn was three years old. He patted me on the knee and said, 'Don't worry, Mama. Pappa is coming back as a young girl in India.' That cracked me up. I doubt that would've been Dad's first choice.

Point is, we don't have control over everything in life. Not even over who we get reincarnated as, or where.

Have handed in the last eps for Show 1. Just praying that it gets recommissioned now.

I do keep thinking about the what ifs . . . and what if I had enough money.

Friday
DAY 277

Feeling a bit down and vulnerable today. Lovely walk with Husband, and coffee in the park, but constantly feeling hurt that the Lastborn doesn't seem to need me anymore. I realise this is what being an 18-year-old is all about. And her personal motto has always been 'I can do it'. But still, it hurts.

Does make me feel bad for the way I treated my own mom, but also, my mother got shitfaced every night, whereas I've tried my very best *assumes Saintly Blessed Virgin Mary expression and waits to get Mother of the Year Award*. Feel a bit let down. Feel like I may as well have been getting plastered every day. Also know, though, that this is a normal process for kids. They have to separate from us, not want to spend time with us and think we are embarrassing. It's part of the deal.

Not easy though.

Have a script to get in for Show 3 and that's it.

Am sort of at a loose end because I'm not used to having any free time. Normally, am working 12 hours a day, six days a week.

Saturday
DAY 288

Now that I have time off from work (basically no work), I can turn my mind to other projects. We had no joy from the Final Draft competition for Letlapa's script, so I gave him director Gavin Hood's email address to ask him if he'd be interested in making the film. (FYI, Gavin Hood is the director/writer who won the Oscar for the film *Tsotsi*, and he has made a few stunning films since then.) I emailed Gavin a year or so ago, but my email was so cringey and clearly I did not know what I was talking about, so he just ignored me. I can't judge him, because I do the same with people who message me out of the blue asking if I'll work with them on their book/TV series. Hopefully, he won't ignore Letlapa.

Later: Gavin replied to Letlapa *tout de suite*! He's very sorry but he won't be able to take on the project *nywe nywe nywe*. But I didn't expect him to. All I wanted to do was to plant the seed. I still firmly believe that Gavin is the right person to direct this film and I hope this bears fruit eventually. Or perhaps he will casually mention to another famous film director friend, 'Oh, I was sent this amazing story, you have to make it into a movie.' And the rest will be history.

Yes. You can see why I write for soapies. I have a very rich fantasy life.

Sunday
DAY 279

Matric dance went well. The Lastborn looked . . . I honestly don't even have the words for how spectacular she looked. Little Brother took the most breath-taking photos of her. He is the photographer of the family and takes quite amazing pictures at all our events.

I tried out the new light MCC champers from Woolies at the Lastborn's pre-pre drinks. Very, very delicious. But then I drank a glass of the normal stuff at her friend's house and came back and finished the rest of the MCC.

The great thing was that the first glass of the MCC didn't make me feel tipsy or anything. I think I've found my drink.

Yes, I did drink quite a lot, but I had a good excuse: I had just found out that the Firstborn had an altercation with the oak tree in my car. It will cost thousands to fix. He also hadn't thought to mention it. After being told off, the Firstborn was sulking in his room and wouldn't help with any fetching and carrying or setting up for the pre-pre drinks, and the Lastborn spoke to me like I was a particularly thick ladies' maid. I ended up in tears. It was all a bit too much.

I don't feel an enormous amount of difference between boozing and not boozing, to be totally honest. I have put on weight, and I've turned into quite a painful judgie person when I'm at events. I definitely did need to take a break, but it didn't turn out to be the be-all and end-all that I thought it would be.

I watched a guy's TikTok that talked about the five stages of grief that follow giving up drinking, and that trying to moderate = denial. Perhaps. Time will tell.

Monday
DAY 280

Happy V Day. No, not Vagina. Valentine's Day.

Started off with a migraine so took pills at 3.30 am. Got up to give the Lastborn her V-Day pres before school, and then went back to bed until 8.30. Feeling so out of it, had to have a little nap this arvie.

Things I am grateful for:

- Syndol!

My Valentine's Day blog for this week:

Day of Lurrrrrrve

It is Valentine's Day on Monday, a day much despised by the Husband but one that I force him to celebrate. I have a thing about celebrating these days. I do not care how commercial they are, because I grew up with a father that was the most unsentimental person ever. He once was incredibly proud of himself because he remembered to buy my mother a birthday card – only problem was that he forgot to write anything in it. Yes, dear Reader, he gave her a blank card. My mother laughed, I did not.

I also have a new appreciation of these occasions, having been deprived of fun stuff for the last two years, so yes, I have high hopes for this year's day of lurrrrrve. The Husband, despite his dislike of V Day, is a great gift buyer. One year for Valentine's Day he bought me a Laura Ashley dress from Reminiscene (that fab vintage store in Melville). It fitted like a glove. I loved it so much, I wore it for my publicity photos for my third book, *Delilah Now Trending*.

Have I ever told you the story of how the Husband and I met? It was at the University of KwaZulu-Natal's drama department in Pietermaritzburg. I was a third-year drama student, he was a fresher, having spent two glorious years in the army. We had to do a kind of induction for the first years, so I was dressed as a dominatrix, in a corset with fishnets (obviously – just what the first years needed), and my friend Tombie Auret was dressed as a clown. I was sitting on top of a wall downstairs in the green room of the fabulous Hexagon Theatre in Pietermaritzburg, casually cracking my whip. The Husband spotted me and, rumour has it, decided that I was the woman for him.

We circled each other for the better part of six months (he was dating someone else at the time – a gorgeous blonde) and then finally got together properly during a touring production of *Macbeth* and *Things Fall Apart* (I was Lady M, he was Macduff). Fun fact: we had a fabulous young director called Vee Baxter who organised the production, which was massisvely exciting for all of us, and Vee might actually teach the daughter next year.

We were absolutely mad about each other and could be found to be – in the words of Mammy Keyes in *Again, Rachel* – 'ateing the face off each other' in various venues all over the Hex (belated apologies to all our friends who had to witness this). Later on in the year, the Husband was cast as Rodin's *Thinker* in the dance programme and had to be covered in white paint and sit semi-naked on stage every night (yum!) while I danced, and naturally, I would offer to help him put on and take off his white paint. There was a rather jolly after-party at the end of the run and I fibbed to my parents and said I was spending the night with a friend and then spent the night with Himself.

However, his parents had come down to watch the dance programme and turned up at his flat the next morning. We heard a flatmate saying – in a high-pitched, panicked voice – 'Let me see if he's awake.' Arghhhhhhhh! His parents did not know about me and had never met me, and I certainly did not want to meet them like that. There was only one solution. He bundled me into the cupboard and threw my clothes in after me.

He robotically greeted his parents while I tried not to make a sound in the cupboard and wriggled my way into a jersey so that I wouldn't be completely starkers if I were discovered. His parents had never seen his flat and were exclaiming over the size of the room. Next thing I heard his mother say: 'Oh there's so much cupboard space.' At this point I was praying to the patron saint of sluts that I would not be discovered. The Husband leant against my cupboard and opened the one next to it. 'Yes,' sed he, 'Loads of cupboard space.'

After what felt like ten years they left.

Best cure for a hangover ever.

Afterwards the flatmate said: 'Wow, I just thought your parents were very chilled about the whole situation.' And later on, when they had heard the story, my MIL said, 'He was so out of it, I was worried he was on drugs.'

Yes, everyone did hear the story later on because our best man related it at our wedding.

Tuesday
DAY 281

If the Husband tells me I look 'nice' one more time, I will punch him in the face. There have to be better adjectives out there.

Wednesday
DAY 282

Had insomnia last night after strong coffee I drank with Amy H yesterday. But she gave me some good advice and echoed what I had been feeling – that I am a doormat and a martyr, and I need to enforce some boundaries. This morning I went off to chat to the new mums at Kingsmead. Alex Bouche, who is the marketing director, asked me to be a literary advisor for KBF22. We're also going to try rope in Sue (Nyathi – fabulous author friend), so that's all rather wonderful.

Had a long convo with Big Sister, who offered to help out with the money to send the Firstborn overseas. She is his godmother and could hear that I'm on the verge of killing him. I really do have the best siblings. They are so kind.

In my meditation this morning I was getting a strong message of acceptance – I need to enjoy this downtime 'cause it won't last forever and I will at some point be busier than ever. Live in the now, Pammy. Stop calling up thunderclouds from the horizon.

Thursday
DAY 284

Weirdest phone call this morning from someone at Show 2 – would I like to take part in the documentary celebrating the show? Was so flummoxed I said yes.

They axe me, then they want me to come and say nice things about them in a doccie?? I am impressed by their temerity.

Monday
DAY 287

I tried a light red wine from Woolies this weekend. Taste-wise a little bit sour and young – but nice to feel part of the crowd with a glass of red wine that didn't make me feel tipsy. Also had a glass of sparkling vino at the polo yesterday. Went to the pub yesterday afternoon but had a couple of Diet Cokes.

Don't want to fall back into the pattern of drinking all the time. Want to drink mindfully. The object is not get drunk. I want to have had a whole year of not getting drunk, of drinking mindfully. Really considering every glass I have. Making each one a special occasion.

I also don't want my eczema and skin issues coming back.

What I have realised, though, from this whole journey (I think it's about 9.5 months now) is that the not drinking can become a compulsion. You can start parroting all the stuff you've read in the books. Stuff you don't necessarily agree with.

Also, I have realised that me giving up booze was just another way to try and control my world. And it didn't work.

Have just done a whole bunch of research and binge drinking is different from proper alcohol use disorder. That's why I really don't find it difficult to stay off the grog for long periods of time.

I am now devouring a book called *Drink? The New Science of Alcohol and Your Health* by Professor David Nutt, who tells you all the awful things about booze so you know the risks, but also owns a wine bar with his daughter.

See! It's all about balance!

Tuesday
DAY 288

Stressed about money but am loving having time to do stuff, to be a mom, to work on my novels.

Have the completely bonkers interview for Show 2 tomorrow. Painted my own nails to save money. They look fine if you don't look too closely.

Am now taking off my moustache and a rather luxuriant beard.

So weird to have all this great book stuff happening but at the same time the constant anxiety about the kids and about money and this country.

Russia has invaded Ukraine. People are talking about World War III, so that's jolly. It's like the pandemic was not enough. Ugh. Am wondering if we should be sending the Firstborn to the UK under the circs.

Things I am grateful for:

- That I don't live anywhere near Ukraine.

Wednesday
DAY 289

Did my interview this morning for Show 2, but it was so hard pretending that my relationship with them is wonderful that afterwards I wanted to cry.

But this is me we're talking about. So I did not cry. I just wanted to.

Thursday
DAY 290

Had a glass and a half of champers at All About The Dress last night. Also, served behind the bar. The great thing is I only had half a glass of the one champers – was too sweet – gave it to the Firstborn and then drank another glass, and that was that. I could've had another glass after the event but didn't feel the need.

All About The Dress is a fantastic occasion at the Lastborn's school where they model their matric dance dresses for the school but with no hair or make-up – hence why it's all about the dress. Each matric is accompanied by a grade 1, and frankly the grade 1s think it's all about them. And they could be right. They were beyond adorable.

Have been reading more and more stuff about binge drinking as well as gobbling up this book by Prof Nutt. I've defs been barking up the wrong tree. I am a binge drinker: I am someone who likes to drink socially and who has no trouble controlling herself normally with booze.

The issue here is that it's a slippery slope and I could've slipped into alcohol use disorder if I had carried on. So I'm glad I've taken this journey, and a dry month every year is probs a v good idea.

If I moderate now, then I won't have to give up booze in the future.

I remember my Auntie Joyce, who was the one auntie who didn't smoke and drink (and therefore did not die of cancer). She used to allow herself two whiskies. After that she said she got silly.

So, it is possible.

Friday
DAY 291

Our copies of *Chasing Marian* arrived yesterday, they look gorgeous!

Drank two glasses light champers last night and a very cheap and nasty glass of red wine at Exclusive Books at Boykey Sidley's launch for *Beyond Bitcoin*. Could've had another glass of red but that was enough for me.

Was lovely that they had vino at the launch. I am clearly a lightweight, though, who can't take booze. Even drinking light champers was probably one glass too many for me.

However, I knew my limits and stopped after one glass of red wine, whereas the Husband carried on. Good chat with writer friend Georgie and her husband, actor Ter, about binge drinking. G barely drinks at all. I admitted quite freely to them that the only reason I really drink is to keep in with everyone else. If I'm with people who don't drink, I'm happy not to drink. We snuck off to look at the copies of *Chasing Marian* in the bookstore and took some pics with Boykey's wife, author Kate Sidley, who will be interviewing us at our launch. Pretty tacky to do this at someone else's book launch but I knew Boyks would understand.

Monday
DAY 294

The girls won their water polo matches yesterday and got the plate and medals. We came ninth overall, huge step up from our last finishing position of 22!! The Firstborn came to watch the Lastborn play her final match yesterday, where she scored a goal or helped score a goal or whatever. She also scored a beautiful goal in the first match. I was massively proud of her and had a glass of bubbly to celebrate, and really the one was enough. But these were the thoughts going through my head:

- ✔ They've opened a bottle for me, I really should have another glass
- ✔ I don't want another glass; one is actually enough.

The more I manage to just have one or two glasses, the prouder of me I am because the hardest thing is to try and moderate. Might need to get 'Thanks, but I've had enough' tattooed on my forehead.

When we got home, I thought of having a glass of red wine with the Husband but then I thought 'Why?' It was a really ordinary table wine, why waste my alcohol allocation on something so blah? I had sparkling water and tea and that was great. I'm like that with coffee too and sweets – I won't waste my allocation on substandard stuff.

I like what Prof Nutt has to say about alcohol being a dangerous drug that needs to be treated with respect. We need to drink the least amount of alcohol to get the best effect, and not just toss cheap crap down our throats at every occasion simply to get blitzed.

I still don't know what's happening with work, which is majorly stressful, but I am so enjoying having weekends and downtime. God, it is so beautiful that I don't want to go back to working like I was.

Practically no one was even bothering with masks at the water polo or the book launch last week, and it was very nice to be free of them. My mascne seems to be clearing up.

The war in Ukraine rages on. Putin is now threatening with nuclear stuff so that's lovely. Just googled how to survive a nuclear attack and the best places to be in the event of a nuclear war and Cape Town made the list, so that's encouraging. Silver lining and all.

I'm interested in the psychology of wanting to go to war after a pandemic. Is it just because everyone's feeling so pissed off that they now feel the urge to fire missiles at each other. You know, a bit like how toddlers start fighting if they've been cooped up?

ACT IV

Trying to not get shitfaced

(March-ing on into the future)

MARCH

Wednesday
DAY 296

Tried to have a little celebration with the offspring last night for Shrove Tuesday and the pub day of *Chasing Marian*. (Yes, I also thought that was a day you went down to the pub, which I suppose for a lot of people it is, but what it's actually short for is publication day.) Efforts to celebrate were pointless. Lastborn started getting lippy after about ten minsutes, and Firstborn went off in a huff before the pancakes were ready.

I DO NOT LIKE MY CHILDREN.

At least I have lovely nephews and nieces.

People used to make much more of a fuss when I first got published. This is book number four and I kind of got a cursory 'Ja, well done, hey Bam Bam.' (Bam Bam is my childhood nickname.)

No flowers, no champagne, zip. Feeling underwhelmed by my family's response.

Friday
DAY 298

Slightly upset – okay, *very* upset – by the tone of the conversation I had today in the story room with a group of people I usually respect. I spoke about how a Zimbabwean friend (with a legitimate work permit and a master's degree) was returning to Zim because of the xenophobia she's been experiencing. Well, did I get jumped on from a dizzy height. I was told that Zimbabweans are the ones committing all the crimes in the townships and that this guy heading Operation Dudula is right. Yikes. Found the attitudes quite repulsive. Obviously, although I was born in South Africa, I grew up in Zimbabwe and I still have family there, so I do feel defensive when people start attacking Zimbabweans. I really did try to see their point of view. But later decided, 'Nah, fuckit, they're being horribly xenophobic, and I'm not interested.'

Odd thing happened yesterday: a guy who used to live in this house, like 50 years ago, and who now lives in the US came to visit. (No. This is no relative of the 80-year-old who came to visit for his oak tree.) I took him and his wife around the house. Was so amazing. He used to have a treehouse in the oak tree, exactly where I am planning my posh writing treehouse.

Mentioned my posh treehouse to the Husband.

Husband: No. You will ruin the view. Put it in the back garden.

Was about to argue but then realised we have no money to build a birdhouse let alone a treehouse, so shut my trap rather smartly.

Monday
DAY 301

Quite a boozy weekend – a few glasses of red wine on Friday night, which, I have to say, I thoroughly enjoyed, and then two mimosas yesterday at a family brunch.

This week I might drink at the book launch on Thursday and the cocktail party on Friday, but let's see.

Listened to something on the radio this morning – a funny ad about a woman marrying a guy who had already peaked. He'd been in the first team rugby and cricket at school. Really do hope I haven't peaked and that it's all downhill from here. Ghastly thought.

People are dropping like flies around us. Heart attacks and aneurysms. Can't help feeling like it's linked to Covid. Had convo with the Husband this morning about what I would do if he dropped dead. Think

I'd bugger off and live on Rhodes or Corfu or in Mauritius or somewhere. I'd want to be by the beach. He was slightly concerned about how happy I looked at the idea.

The Lastborn is going with some girl to her matric dance at one of the sister schools. Too nervous to ask if she's also coming out, or if she's just trying to make a point (which is more likely – she loves a protest), or indeed if she just wants to jol with her mates at the other school. Was informed by a dear friend that apparently all the kids are pansexual now or something. This is not like having a thing for Le Creuset pots BTW, it's about falling in love with the person's intellect not their gender. The Lastborn thought she'd spend two grand on a suit. I quickly disabused her of this notion, particularly as I'm slightly bitter that I have no idea who her partner is and have not been invited to the pre-drinks. I told her if she's so desperate to wear a suit, she can wear the Firstborn's one from his matric dance.

Big Sister and her husband paid us a surprise visit on Friday night. The Husband told them he had no booze in the house, so the brother-in-law rocked up with a bottle of white wine, two bottles of delicious red and a bottle of whisky. I was make-up-less, in an ancient dress with my greasy hair tied up because I had been in a Zoom story meeting all day and then had to write a script. Maudie was shocked and was trying to think of a nice way to say how bloody awful I looked but instead told me that I looked 'tired' and perhaps I should think about cutting my hair short as she loved that style on me.

I drank two to three glasses of vino, but as soon as I started feeling a bit merry, I stopped and had a cup of tea and some water. I still did have a bit of a racing heart from the red wine, but I felt fine the next day. That's kind of what I'm after, the ability to STOP and know when I've had enough.

The war in Ukraine is still raging and the Russian government is busy cracking down on its protesting citizens. Our government is firmly on the Russian side, which is a bit vomitous. But hey, who am I to talk? I'm the one who did that video for a show that ghosted me, and I worked with Iago, so I shouldn't really be commenting.

We've had a few days with no Covid deaths. We think we're now in the recovery phase of the pandemic. Also, it was the second anniversary of the first Covid case a couple of days ago. Two whole years of this nightmare. Ugh.

Autumn now and the weather is starting to cool down. Hopefully it will start to rain less.

Thursday
DAY 304

Lots of exciting stuff happening professionally. Had a meeting about turning Qarnita's first book, *Being Kari,* into a limited drama series. Not sure if anything will come of it, but I would be so happy if it did. I am a huge fan of her books and that is one of the things I so desperately want to do – adapt SA books for TV.

(Just putting it out there into the universe.)

Radio host Jenny Crwys-Williams left a message for me. I called her back. It was about a possible cocktail event with us for *Chasing Marian.* She thought I was Sam Cowen for the first ten minutes of the conversation, which was hilarious. Am also thick in the organisation for the Kingsmead Book Fair, plus I'm on the PTA, and we are in the middle of story workshops for Show 1, and I have a script to write for Show 3.

I love being busy.

The Lastborn's play opens tonight. Need to get flowers to her. She has decided she wants to try out for Gauteng Schools Water Polo. Felt excessively irritated that she wants to do this when already she has so much on her plate – and she has her goddamn provincial colours for Open Water Swimming already, so whyyyyyyyyyyy?? Tried to gently suggest that she really, really doesn't need to put herself under that pressure in her matric year. She ignored me. I can't really be irritated because she's just like me.

Stage 4 loadshedding at the moment, which is so lovely.

I had the sudden realisation about living in the moment. You never know if you'll have these particular cool experiences again, so you have to savour them and enjoy them.

Pissed with rain the whole of yesterday. Very much a season of mists and torrential fucking rain that pours through the ceiling.

Things to be grateful for:

- That the Vaal Dam is full (trying to look on the bright side).

Sunday
DAY 307

Had a glass of red wine at the book launch on Thursday. Amy H was in convo with Catherine Jarvis, author of lovely YA novel *The Swim Team*. Exciting that they do now have wine and drinks at the launches, although no snacks. The wine wasn't my favourite, but I still drank it – and much faster than Amy H.

Then drank a glass and a half before the Lastborn's show on Friday night. A very immersive and rather delicious production of *A Midsummer Night's Dream*. The Lastborn acted a small part, was an assistant director on it and composed a piece of music, which she played in one of the fairy segments. This was all achieved while also being swimming captain, house captain and playing first team water polo.

When the play finished on Saturday, she hurriedly got changed and then rushed off to the matric dance, which meant that she missed her cast party. I was not happy with her. She tries to do too much and then misses out on things she would really like to do. But how can I reprimand her?

She is her mother on steroids. It's extremely unpleasant to see your less admirable qualities coming out in your children. When I was younger, I thought my workaholism was a virtue, I don't anymore. I think it's just another of my addictions, a way to try and make myself feel worthy. Spoiler alert: it doesn't work.

Also, yesterday, we were on our way to Blind Tiger when a woman T-boned us outside the son's old nursery school. She went through a stop street and her car is pretty fucked as a result. The Husband leapt out of the car and started shouting at her, so I had to calm him down. I was shaking afterwards, and a kind neighbour came out and gave me some sugar water. I thought this other driver was in her twenties when she started to cry, but she's 37. I sat there rubbing her back and then complimented her on her skin. I know it was probably inappropriate, but her skin *was* gorgeous. She was wearing these small booty running shorts and had her dog and a box of wine in the car. She has an amazing figure and did look like a twenty-something and seemed fragile.

After this excitement, we then went to Blind Tiger, and I drank a small carafe of red wine with some sparkling water. I think it was about 200 ml of red wine. Mavis, the bartender, was beyond thrilled because it's the first booze I've drunk at the pub since I started my sober curious journey. Did calm my nerves a bit but still felt shaky for most of the evening. Not a pleasant experience and really not what we need right now.

Book launch for *Chasing Marian* on Tuesday. Am planning on doing crazy rock-chick hair. Need something to amuse myself as everything is pretty grim at the moment.

The coffee guy, Max – he ran the coffee shop at the son's prep school – well, he was gunned down a week or so ago. Thought it was a robbery gone wrong but turned out to be a xenophobic attack on Zimbabweans. The perp shot four people. Mmm, hope the people who support the Put South Africans First assholes are pleased and proud.

Max has four kids. He paid taxes. And now he's gone.

Thursday
DAY 311

Happy Paddy's Day! Cold and rainy. Seems appropriate. Usually, I would be going to a pub somewhere for a night on the razzle but those days have passed.

Book launch went off like a dream. They even rolled out the red carpet for us – literally! The launch was packed. Kate Sidley did a beautiful interview, even though it must've been a bit like herding cats trying to interview the four of us as we all talked over each other, laughed at inside jokes and disagreed loudly about when we did what.

We sold 70 books and signed ten more at Rosebank and a bunch at Love Books, so that was fab. Still no overseas deal yet, but the publishing team has been incredible – they have all really gone above and beyond the call of duty for us.

We were all dithering about what to wear. It was supposedly the first time we wore our special *Chasing Marian* T-shirts. Confession: I wore mine to do the interview for Show 2 – I thought I may as well get some publicity out of it for the book after the fuckers axed me like that. What was lovely is that in return for giving her some publicity, Nadia Kruger, who made the Lastborn's matric dance dress, made me this fabulous pale green skirt with shocking-pink tulle underneath – for free. So appreciated as I had no money to buy anything new.

We had been planning on all going to have our nails done together but time ran away from us, and we all had various school and work commitments. I left the story meeting early and was a bit hurt because no one even wished me luck for my launch.

I had a half a glass of wine after the launch. Was very tempted to calm my nerves with one beforehand, but didn't. I'm glad, because it makes me fuzzy-headed. Then drank a glass with dinner afterwards. The Husband very sweetly bought all of us flowers and my family bought about 15 books between them and brought friends along, which was so kind. I was less impressed with the offspring, who didn't even bother to hang around to take a picture with me and sort of slumped in the front row during the launch looking bored out of their skulls. Made me long for the old days when they once played their guitars and sang before my launch and then dutifully asked questions in the Q&A session afterwards. Now they can't wait to leave. Not sure if they were embarrassed or bored, or both?

The next day, we had another book event in Pippa Smith's garden. It was chilly but fun. We then had tea at Schim's and signed each other's books, and then Qarnita and I went to Blind Tiger, and I had about two-thirds of a kir royale that I found terribly strong. Q ordered a pink mimosa. Much better bet – not so strong – but she barely touched it.

All the attention on us was a bit overwhelming, but we really could not have asked for a better launch.

I am exhausted now.

Am waiting for my salary from Show 1, which is taking forever and is beyond nerve-wracking. But at least it's on its way.

I still feel weird drinking at all, like an addict, wanting to drink but watching myself. Trying to drink normally. I do understand why some people say it's just easier giving booze up altogether. Moderation isn't easy.

Sunday
DAY 314

After my last entry the Husband and I sloped off to the pub and had a couple of drinks for St Paddy's Day and we had a good chat. Then on Friday night we saw old friends at Cousin Box's house for a braai. Am feeling particularly proud of myself because I only drank a glass and a half of wine. I could feel like I'd had enough, and I stopped. A friend then topped up my glass, but I poured it into the Husband's glass.

What was a shocker was that my cousin's son explained that a standard glass of wine at a restaurant – 175 ml – is two units of alcohol. It now makes sense as to why one feels so pissed after only a couple of glasses of wine. That's why I like that light champers from Woolies because you don't feel so drunk.

As I sat around the table with my old friends, I had such a wave of nostalgia for the hopeful, young people that we were. Especially, when I think of what that family's been through. Their nephew died by suicide after being sexually abused by one of his sports coaches. It doesn't even bear thinking about.

The point is to never get jaded or stop trying and hoping and working towards whatever success means to you. Because if you do, what's the point? You're just waiting to die.

So, I will keep writing and submitting and striving and hoping that Go See Do makes money. When I start moaning, I think 'At least I'm not in Ukraine.' To see what those poor people are going through. Yikes!

Monday
DAY 315

Human Rights Day today, when we commemorate the Sharpeville Massacre. Thinking of those brave people and the Ukrainians makes me realise I could never be that courageous. Would be on the first plane out of there.

It is also the tenth anniversary of when I received a letter from Louis Greenberg, the commissioning editor of eKhaya, the digital imprint of Random House Struik, to say that he wanted to publish my book *Ms Conception*. I had been on the verge of trying to self-publish and was sitting with artist friend Minky Stapleton at Rosebank Mall when fellow master's student and author Andie Miller walked by and asked me how the book was coming along and then suggested that I send it to Louis. It really was a freakish coincidence that led to my dream of getting published actually coming true. The best part is that Andy was part of the editorial team for the book, and Minky designed the gorgeous cover and went on to design the cover for my third book, *Delilah Now Trending*, and is the cover designer of the book that you are reading right now. She's also an award-winning children's author.

When I did eventually get published, it wasn't as if the book immediately shot the lights out. If I sold 100 copies of the book digitally, it was a lot. It was when Penguin Books and Random House merged and became Penguin Random House, and the South African branch then decided to bring the book out in hard copy in 2015, that my career as an author took off properly.

This idea of people having immediate success is most of the time absolute nonsense. Even people who are young and seem suddenly successful, have probably been child actors or whatever. Success takes hard work – and luck.

Had a really nice day yesterday, wrote three-quarters of my script, cooked a fab meal for the kids and drank a small glass of cheap and nasty red wine last night to keep the Husband company. We sat at our outside bar. I drank very slowly and made it last during supper. It didn't make me feel pissed. Was perfect really.

Going to Little Brother's house for a braai today. They have sold their house and my nephew is out from the UK to say goodbye (to the house). Am just hoping that the offspring do not drink too much. It's my child-of-an-epic-boozer need to control the situation that is making me anxious. Also, the thought that I might have to drive home. Might ask my son if he will be the designated driver today. I don't think he'll mind ,and that'll stop one child from drinking too much.

Have a script to get in today for Show 3 and then workshops for Show 1 for the next three weeks before editing starts. Am trying to scrape money together to tide me over for these two months where I don't earn a proper salary. At least I will be editing and writing for Show 1, which will make up for some of the lost income from Show 2.

I read something by Marian Keyes where she said that when she goes out, she tells herself that all she has to do is NOT DRINK.

I think for someone practising moderation, all you have to do is NOT GET DRUNK. That will be my mantra.

You have to stop and not just continue chucking booze down your gullet.

Yes, I do understand this is not always as easy as it sounds. Especially when the booze seems to literally jump from the bottle into your glass and into your body.

Tuesday
DAY 316

Big Brother's 64th birthday today. He and Del gave away just about everything here and went off to have an adventure overseas and ,really, they seem to be living their best lives. Am v happy for them.

The Firstborn did agree to be the designated driver yesterday. He had to drive my car in the rain and did very well. It was the first time I had ever driven with him – he got his licence last August. I'm afraid I was just too nervous to before and I also didn't want to freak him out by clutching on to the seat and saying the rosary (in the true family tradition). The Husband didn't stop telling him what to do, until he lost it and told his dad to STFU (in not quite those words), and I felt a huge sense of relief because I realise that it's not just me. The Husband can't help himself; we've all got to take the routes he wants to take and drive the way he tells us to.

At the braai, I drank a glass and a half of light champagne and two glasses of red. Had had enough and stopped and had water and tea. Felt a bit buzzy from rich food and alcohol when I got home but reflected that it's no different to how gassy I feel after drinking either Tab or dealc'd sparkling wine all night. Had a surprisingly good night's sleep.

Also, the point about not drinking too much is to leave at a reasonable hour. We left just after six. I suspect the Husband would've stayed and carried on drinking if he could have, but I'm done with that. I had a really pleasant evening and I'd had enough.

I would add that together with NOT GETTING DRUNK, I need to add NOT DRINKING EVERY DAY. That's also a worrisome pattern to fall into and it's very much related to the friends you hang out with.

Have all day meeting today. Grateful for the work.

Wednesday
DAY 317

Because we had to sell one of the bakkies and send the one from Gauteng office to Cape Town, we now use the little car Maudie gave the children to do the deliveries. This means that the Firstborn is deprived of his car for a week and then uses mine, which costs me a fortune in petrol.

I am thinking that if things don't improve by the end of this year, we should just sell the house. We can't actually afford to live here, and I am so fucking sick of having no money. The only problem is I love this house, it feels like my forever house, and I don't want to sell it. We might not have a choice.

Thursday
DAY 318

Feeling better today, no idea why, have no reason to. The weekend is nearly here and, ja . . . life goes on.

In my walk and meditation and all the discussions about death, I just have the feeling how interconnected we all are, that death is just an altered state and that the dead are still with us.

A twitter friend – Kgauza Lecowza – died yesterday. Huge sports' fan, always chatting about rugby, total boykie, but also just a nice, nice guy.

Used to call me his big sister. Often posted clips from music videos – one of his faves was that song from *A Star Is Born*, 'Always Remember Us This Way', which I also love – I often see it on TikTok, and every time I do, it reminds me of him. Feel sad about his passing, but also happy that I knew him.

Kindness wins.

Contacted the insurance guy to see if this bonus on my retirement annuity is payable now. I am going to need a cash injection from somewhere to get through the next month.

Also, had the realisation that this is the size I am and that's okay. I'm not going to starve myself to try and achieve some ridiculous, low weight. I am going to eat healthily and keep exercising and feel beautiful the way I am.

My focus will be on health and feeling strong.

Well, at least until next summer when I put on my bikini and have a freak-out.

Friday
DAY 319

Chasing Marian is 17th in the Nielsen ratings and 6th in SA fiction. I have no idea what this actually means, but as none of my books have charted before, I think this is good. We have also been chosen for the Exclusive Books Homebru promotion. Awesome.

The Firstborn has had an interview for the overseas school, and it looks like he might be going sooner rather than later. We are going to miss him. 🙁

Monday
DAY 322

We are living through one of our hardest periods ever. Financially things are beyond shit. The landlord for Go See Do Gauteng wants to kick us out of our offices – understandably, because we haven't paid rent for a year. We have all the expenses involved with getting the Firstborn overseas and I haven't been earning a proper salary and my first proper one will be at the end of May. All very tough. And no, I do not want to ask Maudie for cash as she has already done enough for us.

I've had a very boozy last couple of days. Thursday night we went to Blind Tiger. I had a mini-bottle of prosecco and then shared a glass of red wine with the Husband. Probably 250 to 300 ml of alcohol.

Friday night I had two large (for me) glasses of red wine – maybe a third of a bottle. Saturday, Maudie was here. Went to Blind Tiger – had a mimosa – half a glass of prosecco and then a glass of red – 175 ml and was buzzing.

The Husband drank a glass of red wine when he got home. I had had enough and didn't have any more.

Sunday – two small glasses of red. I felt okay.

In the news about Ukraine, the Russians are fucked but, in the process, have completely fucked up the country. Who knows how this horror will end?

In personal news, the Firstborn goes over to start as a stooge, or what they call a 'gappie', or gap-year assistant, at a school near Norwich in England. Am glad to get him out of here. Incredibly sick of South Africa at the moment, although the rest of the world feels like a king-sized cock-up too. We have Irish passports (as the Husband says, it's the reason he married me). We constantly debate whether we should be staying here, why we aren't leaving, that maybe we should leave, but that this is our home, and we don't want to. Round and round. And I know we're not the only ones. If people are not planning on emigrating, they're at least thinking of semigrating to the Cape.

Supposed to be warm weather this week but today has started off all cloudy and bleh, so who knows?

Tuesday
DAY 323

Father-in-law's birthday today. He's 79. The Husband and I got engaged at his 50th birthday celebration. The theme was something to do with sports and I wore a truly heinous pair of tartan leggings and should've in all fairness been arrested by the fashion police. My aunt's company made my engagement ring. I had it remodelled about twenty years ago and I almost never wear it now as the Husband has brought me several other rings since. I remember my mother-in-law saying towards the end of her life (and she died young) about how she couldn't be bothered getting more jewellery as she only had so many fingers to wear all the rings she possessed. That's why it is kind of fun remodelling what you have. I also like passing my jewellery on to the Lastborn. I get a lot more pleasure from giving gifts than from receiving them these days.

Wednesday
DAY 324

I am in a surprisingly good mood. Not sure why. Even though finances are dire, I am enjoying the stuff I'm doing. Was thinking of hitting the pub tonight, but I do have to ask myself why I want to go to the pub. I think it's habit. Also, I do love a glass of red wine. I wish I didn't, but I do.

Huge realisation last night that although being a bestselling author and whatnot would be wonderful, what I really want is MONEY. Lots and lots of money. And no, don't give me that 'it's easier to get through the eye of a needle than for a rich man to go to heaven' schtick. I call bullshit on that. Money is gooooooood.

I also want money that just comes to me. I don't want to have to spend hours and hours working for it. I've done that, now I just want the free money. I want a big, fat advance for something I've already written, I don't really care which piece of work it's for. Any of them. Just send cash.

That is what I am manifesting:

MONEY . . . pouring into my account.

APRIL

Friday
DAY 326

April Fool's Day – but hardly anyone is bothering as the world is the joke at the moment. Had really horrible headache for the last few days. Eventually took two doses of Syndol and went to bed to get rid of it. Am v worried that it is the booze – we went to the pub on Wed night. Seems to happen particularly on cheap red wine. Only the best will do for Princess Pammy. As Prof Nutt says: make every drink count.

I won't drink this weekend and see what happens.

The Husband might have an offer for the Go See Do brochure business from a man we shall call Shylock. It seems like a bit of a mindfuck, seeing that I've been manifesting money coming into my account. Could this be what all those TikToks have been going on about? Probably not. I'm so very tired, I will believe it when I see the oodles of cash in our account.

The Firstborn's had a hiccup with his overseas gig. Hopefully, the man we are paying a vast sum of money to place him at this school will sort it out.

I am at the stage where I would like to sell everything, step away from social media and just go and live a simple life by the sea. Have this very weird feeling that I just don't want to worry about writing or publishing books or promoting anything or ACHIEVING. I just want to live.

I kind of remember this after doing my undergraduate drama degree. We took two gap years and there was an awful lot of fruit picking and nothing to do with drama. It was kind of nice.

Obviously, I went back to performing. So, I'm not sure what this is about. Is it just about doing things that really make me happy?

Writing what I really want to write but not necessarily promoting it? I'm not sure.

I have felt a lot more relaxed this month. Is it because I've gone back to drinking? Is booze my tranquilliser? Possibly.

Would be lovely to have some loot and a guaranteed job for the Husband for the next few years – I think not acting out of desperation would change a lot about how we live our lives.

I keep imagining the life I want. With time and money so that I don't work every weekend. With time and money to travel and visit people.

But also a simple life.

A life not weighed down by too many things and too many employees.

Lots of time at the beach.

Lots of time for reading and creating and beautiful exercise and helping people.

That's the life I envisage.

No, I have not been smoking weed.

Sunday
DAY 328

Grim, rainy weather today, which is most unlike Joburg for autumn.

Just over a month until this journey comes to an end. Not that it will ever come to an end. This booze thing will be something I will have to keep an eye on for the rest of my life.

Had about a half a glass of cheap red wine yesterday with supper and did not want any more. I only want to drink really good wine, am not interested in the cheap and nasty stuff at all anymore.

Took an anti-inflam for my back yesterday – a Voltarin suppository. Have very fond memories of these when I had such terrible mastitis when I was breastfeeding the Lastborn. They really do the trick. Have tried to interest my family in them. They all look at me as if I've suggested something especially perverted. Their loss.

My card didn't go through twice yesterday at Woolies. Tralalala! My salary has not been paid yet and we are still waiting for loot from one of the tourism areas. I have R700 in one account and R800 in the other. But I kind of just shrug and think, what can I do?

Had a very good chat yesterday with the Husband about how wonderful my working life is. For example, this week: I have story meetings for Show 1; we're doing an interview for *Chasing Marian* on Tuesday; on Wednesday I interview author Cathy Kelly; and we're busy coming up with names for the panels for the Kingsmead Book Fair. I feel truly #blessed.

Watched a thing about near-death experiences last night on Netflix. Love and kindness are what matter at the end of the day – and to yourself before anyone else.

I know now that I do not need to be a bestselling author or famous screenwriter – that essentially none of that crap matters if you feel you're doing good, worthwhile work. Maybe I can say that because I have had some recognition and attention. I don't know. But I really don't need anything more, and in fact I find attention kind of uncomfortable. I just want to be a good employee, to do good work, to work on worthwhile projects, to meet interesting people, nice people that are making a difference, to bring some happiness to people's lives.

Monday
DAY 329

Had a delish glass of wine at Il Contadino yesterday. Was this table of young parents next to us getting tanked. Felt a bit wistful. Miss those days of getting a bit pissed with friends. Although did also have the feeling that it could easily tip over into arguments.

The one woman was shitting on the guy who paid, telling him he can't always pay. Methinks the lady was protesting too much since her partner looked positively thrilled that the other guy was paying. Also at the table was the mother of twins. Exceedingly glad my children are grown up.

Another dreary rainy day. The Husband is not feeling well and has just taken to his bed.

Have all-day story meeting, back is still not great. Am feeling very grumpy and out of sorts. Have not been paid yet.

Oh and forgot to mention that there are massive rewrites on Show 3, so no scripts and therefore no money for that.

I see money pouring into all my accounts.

(That's me manifesting)

Also, it's always darkest before dawn.

We have to keep on keeping on.

Reread memoir by Patrick Swayze's wife, Lisa Niemi, about losing Patrick. Gave me chills 'cause I've been with the Husband for 34 years at the end of this year. Cannot imagine being without him. Loving someone means having to deal with the idea of losing them.

The ultimate lesson in non-attachment.

Someone from Show 1 is being horrible to me. Snippy and mean and putting me down in meetings.

Have no idea why.

What other people think of me is none of my business.

What other people think of me is none of my business.

What other people think of me is none of my business.

It's my need to people-please. I need to get over that.

Tuesday
DAY 330

I want to have such a wonderful life that I have nothing to write here, dear diary! Hahahahaha! I'm not kidding. I had a brief moment in 2007 when we had enough money and work was going well and life was good and then it all crashed when we over-extended ourselves by buying this house and two expensive cars and pouring all our money into the B&B.

Remember the 14-room 4-star guesthouse in Melville we used to own? Nearly sank us.

However, the house that we now live in is in a great area and it makes me feel safe. And our dabble with tourism has led to our stuff now. *Je ne regrette rien.*

Actually, I regret quite a bit, but you cannot go back.

I enjoy just being in meetings, shooting the breeze about stories and not having to actually produce anything. It's a nice break. If I had enough money, I would not give two shits about having no scripts to write. Was chatting to the Husband about our lives. I would love us to travel. Maybe do a road trip around SA and write a book about it. Work on the road, but just write scripts maybe?

Everything will be okay.

The national state of disaster has been lifted after two long years. There are still a whole bunch of restrictions in place, but we no longer have to wear masks outdoors.

I feel naked without my mask.

Thursday
DAY 332

Love is what matters, actually.

But what I have learnt is that love includes setting boundaries and asking for what you want.

It's been one helluva week. Interviewed Cathy Park Kelly last night about her memoir *Boiling a Frog Slowly.* It's about an abusive relationship and how she got out of it. It's beautifully written and is doing so well. Am incredibly proud of Karina Szczurek, her publisher and the founder of Karavan Press.

We've been coming up with names for the panels at KBF, which is hilarious, plus we did a radio interview this morning for *Chasing Marian.* Got to get the blog out. The Husband's moving all the stuff from the Gauteng office into our garage and dining room, plus he has meetings. The Lastborn has a netball festival at St Andrew's. The Firstborn is still waiting to hear about overseas job.

Hectic!

Friday
DAY 333

What a week! But I feel like we're moving forward. The Husband put petrol in my car without being asked, which was kind. We've moved everything back to the house and let's see what happens. First prize is these peeps buying the brochure section of the business and the Husband running it for the next year or two – along with his other work and our work on Go See Do.

Am reading travel books and dreaming about writing something like that. The Husband and I defs need an adventure. But it might only happen in 2024.

Very autumnal, first snow on the mountains. Cloudy and cold.

Monday
DAY 336

A month to go until the end of the sober curious journey. Pissing with rain. Rained the entire weekend. Things are beyond horrible at the moment:

1. Had fight with the Firstborn on Friday. He told me to fuck off and I told him not to fucking speak to me like that and he slammed the door so hard it nearly broke.
2. Got horrendously lost taking the Lastborn to netball. She arrived ten minutes before game. Then car that was in accident got a flat and the Lastborn and I left the Husband and ubered the rest of the way.
3. Beatrice was held at gunpoint in Bree and all her money, and her bank card, was taken. She was supposed to be leaving to go home to Zim for her break.

Quite a boozy weekend. When I say 'boozy', I mean I drank from Thursday to Sunday – one to three glasses a day. When I had three, it was spread out over hours with water. Husband poured me red wine last night, otherwise I wouldn't have bothered. Possibly a bit buzzed on Friday night but that was it.

Eczema on foot was essential oil in bath and not booze.

Xenophobia in Joburg at boiling point. War in Ukraine carries on and on. Covid carries on and on and on. Things are horrible. The world is burning.

Having coffee with Amy H now. Needed some cheering up.

Saw arts editor at local paper at coffee shop who had delicious bit of skinner for us. Someone declined to review *Chasing Marian* because s/he has a problem with one of the authors. Convinced that problem must be with Schim or me, as the group decided that the pair of us are most likely to have pissed someone off.

Bwahahahahahaha!

Weird thing happened. After not feeling like having the story I was working on dissected in the meeting for Show 1, I had a call from one of the producers asking me to skip the meeting and assemble breakdowns. Hectically hard work but very interesting.

Anyhoo – odd how I did not want to be in the meeting and then this happened.

MANIFESTATION, people.

It works.

Wednesday
DAY 338

Have horrible flu. Went for a rona test yesterday. First up-the-schnozz one I've ever had. The others were all deep-throats, and made me gag, as deep-throats do. Was expecting a sort of cringey pap-smear experience, but the lady was an expert and it was fine. I once went to the GP for a pap smear instead of my gynae. The way he was rooting around up there it felt like he was doing a spot of gardening. Learnt my lesson and went back to my (female) gynae after that. The nurse had to repeat the rona test as the first one was a dud, so I got two up-the-shnozz experiences for the price of one. These quick ones are like pregnancy tests, and you get the results immediately.

Thanks god I was negative.

Why was I having a rona test? Because we had the Big Bookclub Bash at Exclusive Books, Bedford Centre. I *selflessly* told them they would have to do the event without me.

Schim: We are not doing it without you. Get a rona test and get your bum down here. I will fetch you.

Poor Qarnita had a tummy bug and had to fly up from Cape Town feeling awful, so we were a bit of a motley crew. But the function was lovely. There was not one person we knew (so we felt like proper famous authors) and it was just so much fun. We had radio host Lundi Cavernelis interviewing us, and she revealed which author had written each character, which made the interview even more fun.

What wasn't so much fun was that everyone else's previous books were there except for mine, so I felt like a bit of a tit when the interviewer asked about my books and then I had to say they're available on Kindle, which is possibly a faux pas in a bookshop. Oh well.

Schim also told me that I should value my influence and not promote anything and everything, and she's probably right, but I don't know if I want to be a paid influencer. I like doing it for the hell of it. Also, if someone paid me, I'd have to toe the line and not lick banners[8] and things. I like being silly.

Because I was high on Corenza I didn't have a glass of wine last night. Am really worried that it's alcohol that is lowering my immune system and making me sick. Again, I'm not sure if this is just me being ridiculous or if it's actually a thing.

But was grateful I didn't have booze on top of the Corenza and managed a reasonable night's sleep until the bloody alarm went off at 3 am.

Also, loadshedding from 10 am till noon, which was a slight pain in the ass.

8 The banner-licking thing started at Schim's launch for her book *The Accident* (I am a huge fan of all her books but that one is my fave). Pan Macmillan do banners of their authors' books and I was so taken with this banner that I took a set of pictures of us all licking it. Or maybe I was the only one doing the licking. Whatevs. It then became a thing. And I was also hellbent on getting published by them so I could have my own banner to lick.

The Firstborn and I are still not talking, but he's being very helpful and cleaning the kitchen, so that's something. The Lastborn is totally enjoying life – she won best-dressed at the danceathon (of course she did). So at least one kid is happy.

Thursday
DAY 339

Terrible floods in KZN, the death toll is over 300 and some of the stories are just horrible. A woman was electrocuted when the floodwater rushed into her bedroom. Then awful things on social media telling Gautengers to stay away from KZN. Why are holiday makers being so selfish and going there? Then other posts saying, please come, we need the business. Why are people so nasty on social media? Block, block, BLOCK.

Am still getting by on caffeine and Corenza. Am now as croaky as hell with an irritating cough but am just relieved to have three days off before the onslaught begins. Once I start editing again for Show 1 on Tuesday, who knows when I will get a proper weekend off?

Soooooooo happy that I have work. Hate having to watch pennies so closely. Feels like such a mingy way to live. Beatrice finally got to go away. Weirdly enough I rather enjoy doing the washing. There's something soothing about it. But I'm afraid ironing and I do not see eye to eye. Clothes will remain unironed.

Ukraine sank some big Russian warship last night so that's jolly for them. But I think all the soldiers in Mariupol surrendered so that's not so good.

Lots of peeps apparently going for Covid tests. Not sure what the answer is. We won't be able to practise social distancing forever. But for those who have comorbidities, it's frankly a nightmare.

More rain expected over the weekend. Ugh. Poor KZN.

The Husband just told me about all the gorgeous wine he bought for the weekend. Not sure when I'll be up to drinking it.

It's Maundy Thursday today. To be honest, I do miss the fantastic church services we used to go to where we would enact the washing of the feet. Although I do remember taking the kids one year and the Firstborn was sitting next to an old homeless guy with really gnarly feet and was appalled at the idea of having to wash them and said so very loudly. More than once. I probs will go back to church one day. I miss the ritual and the singing. Not sure what I actually believe anymore.

The Firstborn and I spoke our first words to each other in a week.

Shylock, the guy who is interested in buying the business is going to talk to the Husband next week about it.

I watched this TikTok thing where you have to keep saying, 'I'm so lucky because XYZ happened.'

Here goes.

I'm so lucky:

- That scriptwriting started
- That they liked my breakdowns
- That I've got a script to write
- That I'm a published author
- That we had such a lovely *Chasing Marian* event
- That I wasn't positive for Covid
- That I don't live in KZN
- That I've had no stuff to do for Show 3
- That we got given this business
- That Shylock is interested in this business
- That I get given books to review
- That I've got three days off
- That I have a house
- That I have cats
- That I have a car
- That I have an education
- That I have a family
- That I can work even though I'm ill
- That the towels dried
- That loadshedding will be finished by tomorrow morning.

Friday
DAY 340

The 12th anniversary of Mom's death. She died a year after she was diagnosed with bowel cancer. She had a bowel resection where they chopped the tumour out in April 2009, but she was adamant about not having chemo and she did not want to end up with a colostomy bag. My GP at the time felt that the cancer was systemic, which meant that the chemo wouldn't have worked anyway. We had lost Luce (my mother-in-law) in 2008 after she went through a gruelling regimen of chemo and radiation that basically did nothing, so I wasn't a fan at that point. However, I did try to keep an open mind and we (my three siblings and I) went to the oncologist to see about treatment. My mother got more and more irritated as she listened to the options, none of which sounded appealing. When we left, she pointed to the fancy convertible outside and said, in a very loud voice: 'That's how she can afford that fancy car, by giving people treatment they don't want.'

Which cracked us up.

In many ways it was a wonderful last year of life. We went on safari to Zimbabwe as a family. She went to Australia to visit her sister and some old friends she hadn't seen for years and then she died peacefully at Maudie's place.

On the day she died, her major concern was that we found a good chair for her old friend, Auntie Margie, who had a bad back. She was incredibly brave and only had morphine on that last day.

The morning that I found out that she had passed away, I got up and edited three scripts. Then I went to Maudie's and drank champagne to celebrate Mom's life. As usual self-soothing with work and booze.

Monday
DAY 343

Zimbabwean Independence Day. 42 years ago.

Remembered the first one, all those years ago. We were driving down to South Africa for our annual holiday in Durban, and a crowd of people surged towards us on the road, singing freedom songs and toyi-toyiing. We shat ourselves because we thought we might've got caught in the middle of a protest, and all quickly raised our fists and yelled 'Pamberi Ne Jongwe' ('Forward with the cock' – don't ask, it's the unfortunate Zanu-PF slogan). But it wasn't a protest, it was a party, and the people were so friendly and happy that we heaved a sigh of relief.

We were living in Harare at the time of independence. Just under a year later, my father was transferred to Bulawayo. I remember how it was slightly creepy driving into town and seeing the remnants of the uprising that had happened just before we arrived. The uprising happened in 1981 and the Fifth Brigade started terrorising the communities around Bulawayo just as we moved back to Harare at the end of 1982.

Then an incident happened that finally prompted my father to give in to my mother's pleas to move down to South Africa. He was a manager of a department at the OK Bazaars and one day he came home with a large bleeding gash on his leg. He didn't really want to talk about it but as it turned out he was roughed up at work by someone who claimed to be a bigwig in Zanu-PF. There was apparently a lot of 'do you know who I am?' stuff. In less than a year we were packed up and on our way to Joburg.

My parents lasted six years in South Africa before they moved back to Zimbabwe.

My flu is so much better. Heard over the weekend that Little Brother tested positive for Covid last Tuesday. Does make me wonder if I had it. Not because I saw him, just because it was going around. I almost left the mention of my illness out of my blog this week because I didn't feel like getting any comments about how I should've stayed at home anyway. Damned if you do, damned if you don't. I felt so bloody ill, I would've loved to have stayed at home, but it was a gorgeous function and they had all put so much effort into it, I didn't want to disappoint anyone. We do just need to get on with our lives now. We are not going to be able to protect ourselves forever.

Spent Friday doing washing – I get very excited when it's a sunny day and my washing is going to dry (the tumble drier is broken and there's no money to replace it). Also started feeling better on Friday and had a glass of very delish Raka.

Saturday was spent in bed binging on limited drama series *Anatomy of a Scandal*, which got some truly hideous reviews but turned out to be really engrossing and I-watched the whole thing. Also, I'm Twitter friends with the author so I was glad I enjoyed it. The Husband poured me the last of the Raka – an enormous glass, was far too much. Anyway, that's all I had to drink on Saturday. Then had two glasses of utterly gorgeous Creative Block 3 yesterday.

Have to admit that I did pour a glass after I heard loadshedding would be reinstated yesterday, but stopped after two, and then shoved a couple of Easter eggs and some hot cross buns in my face. Delish.

Our Easter lunch/supper was yum but the atmosphere was a bit blah. Pissing with rain so we set the table in the kitchen. Did conversation starters afterwards, which are always fun and give me insight into what the kids are thinking.

Moderation works for me fine at home. The test is when we go out. We are so broke we just haven't been going out. But time will tell, especially once my year of sober curiosity is over and I have that freedom in my mind.

Speaking of being broke – a friend from my Maritzburg varsity days contacted me on FB to ask me how I was and to congratulate me on how well I'm doing. I whittered on about how well and happy she looked. Her response: I've been booked off from work for burn-out. Ho-hum. I made some comment about the socials but didn't go into my own personal circumstances and how I basically don't have money to fill up my large 4x4, which also has something wrong with the suspension, which I don't have money to fix.

There is often such a chasm between what's going on in private and what we put on the socials. I would love to be off it, but that's just not an option now. It's part of our lives whether we like it or not. A bit like with the booze, it has to be controlled and moderated.

Today I have a script to write – the first script I'm writing for Show 1 after working as a script editor there for two years. Am a bit nervy.

It's also Easter Monday. I did a whole bunch of reading about the myth of Osiris (when I was supposed to be writing said script) and how similar it is to the Jesus story. Although obviously JC was a real person. I do believe something happened with him rising from the dead to convert the apostles, but the virgin birth, the ascension into heaven, I think those were all just a lovely story. His teachings, however, are not.

Weirdly enough, although I do not believe in religion anymore, I am more spiritual, more at peace and believe more than ever that there is an afterlife beyond our realms of understanding.

The Firstborn and I are now speaking but there's this sense that we are all waiting: he for his stuff to be organised, the Husband for the meeting with Shylock and me for money to drop out of the sky (sort of – am not pinning hopes on it).

Wednesday
DAY 345

Insomnia last night. Feeling shit about everything. Feel stuck and don't see a way out. World feels like one gigantic fuck-up. I am literally counting pennies, avoiding buying butter, trying to eke out the cat food. Perhaps need to have a word with Nigel (the cat) to stop vomming up his expensive food. Ah well.

Went for a lovely walk this morning, wonderful crisp sunny morning and at least loadshedding is supposed to be over tomorrow.

Spoke too soon.

The laundry was awash with water when we got back. The drain is blocked and the Husband could not unblock it, so we are now waiting for the plumber. Also, the handle on the Husband's car fell off. Six grand to fix (hahahaha) so now I have to reach across and open the door for him.

Developed a headache as soon as I saw the flooded laundry so popped two Panados and am hoping it's not the sign of a migraine to come.

In good news, I still have a day to submit my scripts for Show 1.

Thursday
346 DAYS
of sober curiosity and about fourteen year's being in debt

Do you understand why I'm feeling so desperate?

Probably the wise thing would've been for us to sell this house and move the kids to government schools. But somehow, we have hung on to both the house and the schools – God knows how! It's been such a struggle, an endless trudge and a juggling of money. I AM SO FUCKING TIRED OF IT.

But also, hindsight is a wonderful thing and I do feel proud of the fact that we managed to give the kids a fantastic education and we live in a great area. But God, it has nearly killed us. I am so ready for some fun, so ready to stop stressing about money.

I spoke to Maudie this morning. They have solar power and water tanks so don't feel the outages in Vic Falls at all. She mentioned how the residents are clubbing together to get the $7k to fix the transformer because ZESA can't do it. It's becoming like that in SA. Apparently, the peeps in Umdloti have realised that they are going to have to fix the roads after the floods because if they wait for the government, all their businesses will have gone under.

Maudie's flying in on Sunday night and flying to Mauritius on Monday. Did feel just the teensiest bit jealous of her life and had to go and write a gratitude list quickly before I became bitter and twisted and full of wrinkles.

A perfect ending for this memoir would be a fab international book deal and a deal from this guy for our business.

Universe, hello? Are you listening??

Friday
DAY 347

Said that loadshedding was going down to Stage 2, didn't bother to check so bloody doorbell went off at 2 am and woke me up.

I wrote about this person ghosting me in the blog this week. Had a bit of a sleepless night worrying over someone reading it and realising who it was about. Then remembered that quote about 'If you wanted people to write warmly about you, you should've been nicer to them.' Or something to that effect. Also, I doubt half those peeps even read my stuff.

Got an extra script to write so at least next month should be okay. The Husband has a convo set up with Shylock for next week. Who knows if anything will come of it? But fingers crossed. We had a quick drink at the pub last night. Kir royale was delish and went straight to my head. Exactly what I needed. Life is not easy at the moment, so I try and find moments of joy in every day.

Mavis, the bartender, is so thrilled I'm drinking again. Told me I was being very boring on the Diet Coke. She does make me laugh.

This is the blog I was talking about:

Going with the Flow

I saw this thing on TikTok recently where it spoke about not forcing things and going with the flow. Yes, I have reached the point where I am now going to TikTok for spiritual advice. I also love the ones where they tell me my angel in heaven with the name beginning with X is very proud of me. Jokes aside, if life has taught me anything (and frankly it hasn't taught me much, I seem to be dumber than ever), it has shown me that there is no point chasing after something. If it's meant for you it will come to you. (*Chasing Marian* is the exception here. We chased Marian and we found her.) And that applies to people as well as work.

I had a friend we shall call Fern. No, that is not her name. I looked out of the window and saw a fern. This is a step up from naming characters after my pets or dead relatives. Now, I thought Fern and I had a pretty good relationship; we used to enjoy gossiping with each other, we always had each other's backs and we did pretty good work together. But something happened and Fern suddenly became distant. I was the one who had to arrange for drinks. I was the one who messaged her. I was the one who charged around there with chicken soup when she was ill. Basically, I was the one doing all the running and she was making sweet FA effort.

Then, not only was she making no effort, but Fern began being very offish to me, to the point that she would put me down in meetings. At first, I felt hurt and I became like a pathetic puppy dog, trying desperately to get Fern to like me, and then I reminded myself of my mantra: 'You cannot make someone love you or want to spend time with you.' I am a bit slow and a chronic people-pleaser so it took me a while to recognise it, but Fern was just not that into me, dear Reader. And you know what, that's okay.

But this did mean that I had to wipe the word 'welcome' off my forehead (who'm I kidding, it's a tattoo) and stop being available when Fern needed something. This was not about being mean, it was about boundaries. PSA: the more bitter and twisted you are over a friend or lover who has let you down, the more of a hold they have over you, so you want to release that shit *tout de suite*. I do a meditation where I send them the white light. No. Not to zap them and hope they shrivel up and die (although if this happens, it happens) but to release them with love from my life. It seriously does work, try it.

This pandemic and all the shit going down on a daily basis in SA (hiiiiii Eskom, here's looking at you, you beautiful f*ck-up) has been a GIGANTIC lesson in non-attachment and life-is-too-bloody-short-don't-waste-it. I now only really want to work on projects that I like, with people I respect. I have no time for assholes. Pre-rona, I would hang on to work with both hands even if it was with people who wiped their feet on that welcome sign on my forehead twice a day. Now, I'm at the point where I release them to the universe. Sometimes in the manner of George Clooney in *Gravity*, where they drift out to space and die, but ja, at least they're gone.

Let's recap what we've learnt during this blog:

- You can't make someone love you
- Send the white light and release the mean people to the universe
- If the white light kills them, so be it
- The critics are not always right
- You only need one asshole in your life and that's your own
- Don't force things, they will come to you when they're ready.

This obvs doesn't mean you can sit on your ass for the rest of your life waiting for everything to come to you, but it does mean that you should not bang your head on a brick wall when there's an open door behind you.

Yes, I saw that on TikTok. Also, your angel is watching over you and is proud of you. Happy reading and Happy World Book Day!

Xxx

Sunday
DAY 349

Husband just paid the salaries for Go See Do into the wrong account, then his car did not start after he took the Firstborn to the police station to have documents certified on Friday and he had to run up to the garage to get help. No luck. Firstborn then fetched my car, and my powerful battery did the trick. Husband then had a sort of weird turn on Friday night. Reminded me of his vestibular migraines he used to get back in the day that were caused by stress and caffeine. Think he is stressed to the max.

Had a couple of glasses of red wine on Saturday night, a kir royale last night at home, which was meh, and will drink with Maudie tonight. But have a shitload of work to get through this week so am not going to go overboard.

Am supposed to be at a five-day workshop for Show 3 this week (unpaid) as well as getting out five scripts for Show 1. I keep putting one foot in front of the other. It's all I can do. It's frankly a miracle I'm not a raging alcoholic at this point.

I also keep researching Best Greek Islands to live on. Corfu gets my vote. It has a literary festival.

Monday
DAY 350

Oprah said something interesting about manifesting. Once you manifest, you let it go. Truth. Meeting with Shylock – the dude interested in the business – everything is still a bit up in the air, he needs more figures and so on. I did not sleep last night and am exhausted.

Tuesday
DAY 351

Feeling much better today, even though the Husband probably doesn't have work for next month. I think we've both realised that there's no point in forcing things or being desperate or begging or trying to bend over backwards or any of that stuff. No amount of worrying or magical thinking is going to change this. What will be will be. Sometimes you get a nice surprise and things go right.

I haven't tried to go to all the sessions for the workshop for Show 3 or tried to make clever comments. I've just done what I can. Drama at work between the different departments. I've learnt not to rush in to try and fix things, but just to sit back and observe with compassion.

God, I am so mature.

Had a lovely walk with the Husband this morning. He's gone out with a mate now for a bit of a knees-up, which is going to do him the world of good and I'll be able to work in peace without any distractions. Suits me well.

Wednesday
DAY 352

Happy Freedom Day!

Hahahaha! No one's feeling particularly happy or in the mood to celebrate at the mo.

Lovely neighbour Boykey Sidley stopped by the house to get ice last night. He said that he and Kate are just going to get pissed as they've had no power since the last bout of loadshedding, which I think was on Friday. Ugh.

The knees-up the Husband went to got a little out of hand so the Husband stayed the night because he was so wasted. That meant I got a broken night's sleep because I thought he was dead in a ditch somewhere.

Covid figures are going up. Apparently 5k positive last night and 83 admitted to hospital. Really hope it doesn't affect the Kingsmead Book Fair, but so be it if it does. Nothing I can do about it.

Was about to send scripts off to channel for Show 1 when I heard that we have to make a whole lot of changes. Ho-hum. Will also be signing into the meeting at 11 for Show 3. Realised that being a people-pleaser at Show 3 never helped, so now I'm just going to do what I can and if they get rid of me, so be it. I can't be in two places at once. Also, the fact that they expect us to be at these workshops but we're not getting paid . . . ja.

Beautiful sunny day. Washing drying superbly well. The Husband hungover to the gills and barely capable of speech. He looks very green, and just looking at him and knowing if that was me, I would be man down for the whole day, head down the loo, makes me exceptionally grateful for the year I've had.

I NEVER WANT TO DRINK TO THE POINT OF PUKING AGAIN.

Never.

Let me go to this fucking meeting.

Monday
DAY 357

Drinking diary:

- ✔ 1 small glass of red on Thurs night. I was feeling completely exhilarated after being called into an in-person meeting for Show 1. It was so scratchy in the morning with everyone speaking through clenched teeth, but then when the whole team were there in the arvie in person, suddenly it was better.
- ✔ 2 small glasses of red on Friday night at home. Another exhilarating meeting.
- ✔ 2 large glasses of cheap red at the rugby. Although it was so lovely being at the rugby, the cheap red wine left me feeling headachy and ill. I only drank the second glass because a dear waiter who was being crapped on brought it to me. Note to self: don't drink because you feel bad. I then had no desire to drink yesterday.

I actually got paid on Saturday so didn't need the Husband to send me money to tide me over, but I have less money than I expected (of course).

I also had a horrible moment after the rugby when I was feeling headachy and ill at home and I started thinking about our financial situation. I had been feeling sorry for an actor I know who's had no work throughout Covid and thinking 'there but for the grace of god go I'. Then I suddenly had this moment of clarity where I thought: 'But you are exactly like him. You are a freelancer. You have no job security. There's no money left in the bond. You have a retirement annuity that'll pay out a pittance in ten years' time. You cannot afford to retire to a Greek island. You are worth more dead than alive.'

(Again, perhaps not the best idea to mention that to the offspring.)

It was a fucking depressing thought.

But then it kind of focused my mind. Because I can't afford to go anywhere else at the moment. I'm stuck here and I need to make the best of it.

That girl I follow on TikTok – the medium – said something very interesting about just before you get what you manifest: you lose that thing. So I'm manifesting money and that's why I'm so broke now. Let's see if it's true.

I have another meeting for Show 1 this morning and possibly tomorrow.

Later: as I had another walk, I realised that part of my sadness is that I don't feel like I gave my kids their dream childhood. We have had money worries that have got increasingly worse since 2008. I'm not sure which child it affected more, as the Lastborn only had four years of plenty before the shit started hitting the fan. I feel like I have failed as a parent, and not because they didn't have an overseas holiday every year, but because of the low-level anxiety it stoked. But I guess one has to just say that I did the best I could with what I had, and hope that they appreciate things like having me at home with them (even if I was always working), that they lived in a beautiful area and went to good schools.

The sadness is that I hoped things would get better, that I would have the time to give them all the things I wanted to give them, but the Firstborn is about to go overseas and the Lastborn is in her last year of school and time has run out and that makes me sad. Ridiculous but true.

MAY

Wednesday
DAY 359

May the fourth be with you! Hahahahafuckingha.

Loadshedding for the next week.

Plus, the Parkhurst generator tripped, or the substation blew up or something, and the lights were out until midnight. Just added to our general sense of doom and gloom. The Husband is ready to pack up and leave.

Petrol for the gennie costs so much, it's honestly like pouring diamonds into the tank, it's so expensive, plus it stinks and it's as noisy as hell. Was nearly asphyxiated by the gas lamp in my room. And yet . . . and yet . . . we are so lucky to have them. Life would be even bleaker without them.

Covid cases rising and, frankly, everyone has zero fucks to give because everything else is just so shitty.

Looks like they're trying to ban abortions in the US.

The world is such a fuck-up. Ugh.

And now I must plaster a smile on my face and go and make up stories in the story room for eight hours. Probably a good thing as I don't want to be left alone with my thoughts right now.

I'm too scared to pay the school fees because once I've done that, I'll have not a whole helluva lot left in my account with which to buy groceries and everything else for the rest of the month.

I also have the Kingsmead Book Fair and I have to do my hair and nails. On social media people think my life is perfect. And what can I say? I don't want to be a Debbie Downer by telling them what it's really like. Plus, I hate people feeling sorry for me, and I know what social media is like. I can imagine the trolls telling me it's my fault for getting into this much debt. Tell me something I don't know, bitch! Also, I did not create Covid or factor in a pandemic that kind of fucked the cat for us.

I am now having arguments in my head with imaginary Twitter trolls. Send help!

Thursday
DAY 360

Two glasses of rather delish merlot last night. Drank it in the kitchen listening to the hum of the gennie. I have this feeling of acceptance that reminds me of the first year of the Firstborn's life when I was just overwhelmed by despair. Not only was the Husband's ten-year-old nephew dying of cancer, but I just felt so trapped. My business was going to hell in a handbasket, I had horrible postnatal depression and I hated being stuck at home, breastfeeding. I had been so brainwashed to believe that breast was best that I refused to give it up and kept it up through the most appalling mastitis and thrush. You probably just thought you could only get thrush in the vajayjay, amirite? Nope. Also in your boobs. It makes breastfeeding just beyond horrible.

This is what I wrote in *Ms Conception* about it:

> You will feel as if you are giving birth all over again, only this time through your nipple and you will pray for the angel of death to come and put you out of your misery.

And I was not exaggerating. With the Lastborn it got so bad, the specialist thought I had inflammatory breast cancer. She also told me this on a Friday so I had the whole weekend to plan my funeral and choose a friend to marry the Husband off to (I was hellbent on finding a sister wife as I knew if I didn't the kids would never wear sunblock). Fun times.

It was only when I accepted that my life had fundamentally changed that it became so much easier. I also accepted that although I wanted to be based at home, I was not a person who was going to be satisfied baking cookies and going to those toddler classes all day.

People were so mean at the first production company I worked at, which did not help with the general depression. The only thing I can comfort myself with is that this awfulness doesn't last forever. We are constantly in a state of flux; the wheel will turn.

Yes, I saw that on TikTok.

We have to accept that this is our life now in SA – power cuts, water cuts, terrible roads, scrimping and scraping and pivoting our asses off.

Yet we have contacts here, we have a house, paid-for cars (as bloody ancient and rickety as they are), one kid finished his education (for now) and the other in her last year of school. And this is our home. We have to be grateful for what we have. Whining about everything is not going to get us anywhere.

I am turning cartwheels at the thought of Beatrice coming back. The thrill of doing all the laundry has worn off.

Aside: I keep trying to add up how many days there are in a year. Was not sure if it was 364 or 365. Had to google it. Sigh.

Friday
DAY 361

Feeling much more chipper today because it's the weekend and I've got some work done. Also, meeting in person really did help. It made everyone more compassionate and empathetic. Some things defs get lost in translation over Zoom.

So my spiritual lady/tarot reader on TikTok with the divine Scots accent tells me that good things are coming my way. I have to believe in myself and find that safe space within myself when I'm feeling attacked or insecure.

I choose to believe her. As the Husband says, if the planets align, our lives could be pretty cool. I am now not only doing the *Chasing Marian* interview at the Kingsmead Book Fair; I am also facilitating a cooking session. As I know how to cook about three things, this is funny. However, it's a book called *The Cooking Husband* and one thing I'm good at is watching men cook.

Mother's Day this weekend and the end of my sober curious journey. I may, after Kingsmead, do a sober month. I'll see.

Weather is warm but milky sunshine is unpleasant. I want glorious blue skies and bright sunshine.

Monday
DAY 365

I have not been drunk once in 365 days.

Have to admit I felt quite down yesterday – Mother's Day. We didn't go out because we really don't have the money. I had reflexology at Life Day Spa, which was lovely and given to me by a Russian woman who looked embarrassed when she admitted to being Russian, as if I was going to shout 'slava Ukraine' or something. Also, when I asked her if she picked up anything from doing reflex on me, her response was: 'I no believe in this rubbish. I have medical background, I only do this on weekends,' which completely cracked me up. Turns out she's got a degree in sports science.

I got a voucher to get my hair and nails done at the Hairdresser and Some, and a whole lot of wine gums, which I love, and that was it. The Husband and Lastborn headed off to water polo training (bloody Gauteng training . . . grrr) so I got woken up at the crack of dawn after not getting much sleep.

Mondays really are just to be endured. I pray for five o'clock when I can bury myself in a book/TV show.

Booze diary:

- ✔ Kir royale at the pub on Fri night.
- ✔ 2 glasses of delish red wine with dins on Sat
- ✔ 2 glasses of delish red wine on Sunday.

Didn't even feel tipsy, was great. That was the positive thing about Sunday – how different last year was to this year.

I have not got drunk for a whole year.

Wednesday
DAY 367

Watched a TikTok about depression that said basically that it's okay to be depressed – we've just lived through two years of a pandemic. That really resonated with me.

It seems like we are going into the fifth wave but deaths are still low, although I spoke to someone this morning who needed oxygen last night and his daughter needed oxygen this morning.

The Husband has started putting out feelers about working overseas. I keep talking about other people bashing their heads against a brick wall when there's an open door behind them. Same applies to us. Perhaps the universe or even our dead mothers are telling us that it's time to leave SA. We might want to stay in SA, but it just might not be possible. We need to make some tough decisions going forward if nothing comes through for us.

Only thing is that every time we think about going overseas, both of us get utterly depressed. Besides the money issue, we love our lives here. I love working on the shows I work on, I love being a published author and our bookish community, I love my house and the area I live in. My life is pretty fucking cool. Also, I'm under no illusions, I doubt people in the book and TV industry are standing there, going: 'Pamela Power! Yes, yes, yes! We've been dying to work with her.'

I have a funny story about this. There was another Pamela Power on the books when I was represented by that big, fancy London literary and film agency. They tried to send me her royalties, I had to tell them that no, I was not Pamela Power the film editor who starred in the series *Bread*. They did not believe me, and even after I left the agency, my agent once again tried to send me her royalties.

ME: I am Pamela Power, the South African novelist and TV writer.
FANCY AGENT: I know who you are!

Reader, she did not know who I was.

So, I s'pose I could go across and pretend to be the other Pamela Power, although I know zip about film editing and I think the other Pamela is about ninety in the shade. I guess I could just say that I've really been good about the sunblock.

Whatever happens, I release it to the universe!

Although, universe, TBH, I really love my house, I love my job, I love my friends here and I love living in SA, so please come through for us.

I steeled myself and sent off queries about this diary to a publisher mate. Let's see what she says. If there's a market for quitlit, I will edit this, if not, it's been great keeping this diary and keeping track of my boozing.

A
WHOLE
YEAR
OF
NOT
GETTING
SHITFACED.

That's huge.

Epilogue

The day after I sent out the query about this journal, I got an email from publisher Annie Olivier at Jonathan Ball telling me that she found my blog post hilarious, and she'd like me to do an outline for a non-fiction book. I had no idea how to write an outline for a non-fiction book so I first broke out in a cold sweat and then hit Google and worked out what I should say in my proposal. I sent it to her, she took it to the team, and two weeks' later I had a book deal with a very nice advance.

The rest of the year was, financially speaking, one of the most stressful times of our lives. Shylock lived up to his (fake) name and his deal to buy the Go See Do business was a bunch of bullshit. But the universe was, or our dead mothers were, listening to us because by October, the Husband had not one but two jobs, and I replaced Show 2 with yet another lovely show.

Chasing Marian turned out to be a bestseller in South African terms, and after no overseas deals dropped from the sky, our publishers decided to release it internationally themselves. Marian Keyes once again gave us the most insane publicity for our international release, and this is what felt like the real win for me. The support we got from her, and the friendship I found with my three co-authors and our insane WhatsApp group that never fails to cheer me up.

It wasn't quite a happy ending, as we still had a very steep hill to climb in terms of our finances but in romance books, and, frankly, in soapies too, we talk about a 'Happy For Now' ending, and that was mine.

PS: I'm writing this six months after I finished the journal. I have still not got shitfaced and that is the best ending of all!

Selected reading list

The Sober Diaries by Clare Pooley
This Naked Mind by Annie Grace
The Unexpected Joy of Being Sober by Catherine Gray
Sunshine Warm Sober by Catherine Gray
Alcohol Explained by William Porter
Sober Curious by Ruby Warrington
Dry by Augusten Burroughs
Quit the Drink Easily by Jason Vale
Girl Walks Out of a Bar by Lisa Smith
Black Out: Remembering the Things I Drank to Forget by Sarah Hepola
Glorious Rock Bottom by Bryony Gordon
Sober is the New Black by Rachel Black
The Sober Girl Society Handbook by Millie Gooch
Drink? The New Science of Alcohol and Your Health by Professor David Nutt
Stories I Only Tell My Friends by Rob Lowe
Rachel's Holiday by Marian Keyes
Again, Rachel by Marian Keyes
amandakudo.com
ailsafrank.com

Helpline

I chose the moderation route, because I'm a binge drinker. If you are, however, physically addicted to alcohol, then this route is not for you. Please get help. You can contact Alcoholics Anonymous South Africa here: https://www.aasouthafrica.org.za/contact/

Acknowledgements

A book appears to be written by one person but that is not the case at all; it really does take a village. Thank you to everyone at Jonathan Ball, especially to Annie Olivier for commissioning the book in the first place (I have not forgiven her, however for moving to the Cape), and to Sibongile Machika for holding my hand through the process and assuring me that although I am a spoilt princess, my struggles are still valid. Thank you to Karin Schimke for her sensitive editing and her fabulous suggestions. What a WOW to be edited by a writer I so admire. My gratitude to the publicity and marketing team, especially Jean-Marie Korff, Mieke Göttsche and Ndizwanga Nemanashi for their hard work in getting the book out there, and to the booksellers who go above and beyond the call of duty when it comes to selling the books. Same goes for all the book bloggers, book clubs and individual peeps who promote our books on the socials. You are AMAZING! Thanks also to my friends and extended family for providing me with so much material (hahahaha) and for playing major roles in the book. Apologies to my *Chasing Marian* co-authors who feature so liberally, soz, but you ARE famous authors. Thank you to my brother, Tom, for my wonderful author pic and to my friend, award-winning author and artist Minky Stapleton for the truly fabulous cover. Big MWAH to my family: Paul, Liam and Ruby (and my real children, Jinx, Poppy and Nigel) who are my *raison d'être*, I love you guys.

And last, but most importantly, thank you to the readers. You are why we write.

About the author

PAMELA POWER was born in KwaZulu-Natal and raised in Zimbabwe. She holds an honours degree in Drama from the University of KwaZulu-Natal Pietermaritzburg and a master's degree in Writing from the University of the Witwatersrand, where she taught for many years. She is the author of three novels, *Ms Conception, Things Unseen* and *Delilah Now Trending,* and is one of the co-authors of *Chasing Marian.* Pamela has worked in the television industry for the past twenty years as a script editor and scriptwriter and is a director of Go See Do South Africa, for which she writes a weekly blog about books, movies, TV and life. Pamela has three cats, two children and one husband. You can find her on Twitter @pamelapower.